HASTINGS
1066

HASTINGS
1066

JONATHAN TRIGG

To the lost housecarles of England, and for everyone prepared to stand in a wall for what they believe in – stabilis! To Maddy and Jack too, because I promised.

First published 2012
This edition published 2015

Spellmount, an imprint of
The History Press
The Mill, Brimscombe Port
Stroud, Gloucestershire, GL5 2QG
www.thehistorypress.co.uk

British Library Cataloguing in Publication Data.
A catalogue record for this book is available from the British Library.

ISBN 978 0 7509 6518 7

Typesetting and origination by The History Press
Printed in India

CONTENTS

ACKNOWLEDGEMENTS

Thank you to David, Sarah, Charlie and Milly, to Nigel, and to Liam for tramping around a castle in the pouring rain. As ever with any book it is a team effort and several people have helped me with proof reading, made suggestions and amendments and corrected mistakes and for that I thank them, and whilst I have of course made every effort to achieve complete accuracy, if there are any mistakes they are entirely my own.

LIST OF ILLUSTRATIONS

as they charged the unarmoured Norsemen and their English allies under Tostig. Also present was Copsi, a trusted lieutenant of Tostig who would survive the battle and be made Earl of Northumbria by William the Conqueror before being murdered by the local nobility just five weeks later.

25 The Norman invasion fleet crosses the English Channel.

26 Dives-sur-Mer, where the Norman fleet assembled in preparation for the invasion of England.

27 French cavalry horses are disembarked on the English coast.

28 Bishop Odo blesses a meal at the French camp.

29 Pevensey Beach. Here at what is now called Normans Bay, William and his army came ashore. The bay is long and sheltered and perfect for landing troops and supplies.

30 Stretching away for several miles inland from Pevensey Beach are the tidal flats, drained now, but in 1066 they were not ideal territory for heavily armed soldiers and their horses.

31 The old Roman fort of Anderida (modern-day Pevensey). Garrisoned by the Romano-Britons after Rome's departure, it was destroyed by a Saxon raid. William occupied it and built the first Norman keep inside the Roman walls and ditch.

32 Pevensey Castle. The medieval keep was built on the old motte and bailey wooden construction first placed there by William's carpenters.

33 Moving away from Pevensey, William marched his army along the coast to the far better site of Hastings. Here he ordered the erection of another fort.

34 This scene from the Bayeux Tapestry did not shy away from showing the Normans burning the houses of locals in the Sussex countryside. It was a pattern they would continue throughout England and would reach its zenith – or rather, nadir – in the Harrying of the North.

35 The routes taken by William and Harold to Hastings.

36 Hastings today.

37 The gatehouse of Battle Abbey. In 1070 Pope Alexander II ordered William to do penance for killing so many people

52 An artist's impression of the battle. It shows the possible steepness of Battle Hill before it was levelled out with terracing and the building of the Abbey.

53 Unarmoured and relatively inexperienced select fyrdmen thought they had the Normans beaten and ran down the hill after them. The Norman cavalry rallied, turned and cut them off. The desperate English tried to form a new, mini shield wall, but to no avail, and they were butchered to a man.

54 Unlike the English the Normans had a large number of archers; one of them is shown wearing mail armour and hence is of relatively high social status.

55 Bishop Odo urges on the Norman soldiers, while in the background a Saxon is speared by a horseman.

56 The battle nears its end, and Harold's brothers, Earl Leofwine and Earl Gyrth, are killed.

57 King Harold's death at the Battle of Hastings, the most controversial scene from the Bayeux Tapestry. Is Harold the figure struck by an arrow, or the one chopped down by the sword of a cavalryman? Or both?

58 A Victorian depiction of the Battle of Hastings.

59 Waltham Abbey Church. This ancient church and its peaceful grounds sit in the midst of the modern town. Part of the wall nearest to Harold's gravesite is from the original Saxon building.

60 King Harold II's memorial in the grounds of Waltham Abbey church. The plaque reads: 'This stone marks the position of the high altar behind which King Harold is said to have been buried, 1066.' Every 14 October people gather here to remember him and lay flowers.

61 The memorial built to mark the spot where King Harold supposedly fell.

62 The ruins of Berkhamsted Castle where Archbishop Stigand brought the Atheling Edgar and the Earls Edwin and Morcar to submit to William. The Anglo-Saxon Chronicle considered 'it was a great piece of folly that they had not done it earlier.'

INTRODUCTION

In AD 410 the Roman province of Britain was under attack from waves of seaborne Saxon, Pictish and 'Scotti' raiders. Unable to protect the island, the Emperor Honorius wrote to Britain's leading citizens instructing them to look to their own defence. Invasion and war consumed the province as imperial Rome's 400-year-old British adventure finally came to an inglorious end. Roughly a century later, a Saxon warrior named Cocca looked down into a lush, green valley nestled among the South Downs, some nine miles from the Romano-British city of Noviomagus (modern-day Chichester). The valley was well watered by a tributary of the nearby Rother River, and the surrounding chalk hills sheltered it from the wind. Leading his band of followers and their families down through the woods of oak, beech and elm, Cocca decided this was the place they had crossed the cold northern sea to find, and built a village there to which he gave his name – 'Cocking', as it became known.

As the years passed, these men who were once sea-pirates let their swords and spears rust, used their battleaxes to cut back the forest instead, and turned their strong arms from rowing dragon-ships to ploughing the rich soil of their new farmsteads. Cocca's descendants even forsook the worship of Woden, the one-eyed grey god of their forefathers, and bent the knee to the

1. The Cocking Memorial pillar was erected to celebrate the millennium. It commemorates significant events in the history of this quiet West Sussex village.

new religion of Christianity, for which they built a church. Saxon chieftains and petty kings warred, politicked and married, and eventually Cocking became part of the mighty and powerful kingdom of the West Saxons – Wessex, ruled by the royal line of Cerdician kings.

Life was good, the summers were long, the winters mercifully short, the crops grew tall and the flocks multiplied. Then, almost 300 years after their own ships beached on the shores of this island, Cocca's Saxon heirs listened to their priest in his pulpit preaching of an atrocity far to the north carried out by a new wave of raiders. Off the rugged coast of Northumbria, the holy island of Lindisfarne, previously home to both Saint Aidan and Saint Cuthbert, had suffered slaughter and robbery as the Viking age dawned. The Anglo-Saxon Chronicle said of the attack:

AD 793: This year came dreadful fore-warnings over the land of the Northumbrians, terrifying the people most woefully: these were immense sheets of light rushing through the air, and whirlwinds, and fiery dragons flying across the firmament. These tremendous tokens were soon followed by a great famine: and not long after, on the sixth day before the ides of January in the same year, the harrowing inroads of heathen men made lamentable havoc in the church of God in Holy-island, by rapine and slaughter.

The villagers of Cocking may have thought this raid was a long way away, but five years earlier there had been one a lot closer to home, just along the coast to the west at Portland in Dorset:

AD 787: This year King Bertric took Edburga the daughter of Offa to wife. And in his days came first three ships of the northmen from the land of robbers. The reeve then rode thereto and would drive them to the king's town, for he knew not what they were, and there was he slain. These were the first ships of the Danes that sought the land of the English.

For the next 250 years Anglo-Saxon England was plunged into chaos and war as the kingdoms of Northumbria, Mercia and finally East Anglia were all swallowed up by the invaders. Alcuin, a Northumbrian Saxon scholar in Charlemagne's court at the time, wrote:

Never before has such terror appeared in Britain as we have now suffered from a pagan race … The heathens poured out the blood of saints around the altar, and trampled on the bodies of saints in the temple of God, like dung in the streets.

Cocking stayed safe and peaceful nevertheless, shielded by the vastness of the primeval Andredsweald forest to the north. Occasionally, young men in search of adventure would leave the village and go off to fight for their king, be it Egbert, Ethelwulf, Ethelred, Athelstan, Edward or Alfred, and all freemen in Cocking were, naturally, members of the ancient Saxon citizen militia, the *fyrd*, but the war never touched the home of Cocca's people.

Life went on at the same pace it had for centuries, marked by the passage of the seasons and the intimate details of village life – births, deaths and marriages, and all the gossip that went with them. Some new families moved into Cocking, and some old ones either moved out or died out, but overall little changed. Cocking was not rich but it had prospered enough to build a hall where the villagers would gather on feast-days to celebrate, drink and dance. Some villagers had enough money to buy a few slaves, usually dark-haired Welsh, but most of the populace were smallholding freemen and artisans. Cocking's fields now totalled over 1000 acres of prime farmland, five mills for grinding corn, and good woodland for timber, and by 1066 this wealth made Azor, the latest of Cocca's line, an important man in Sussex and the southern earldom of Wessex overall. He was a thegn, one of the ranks of men who held their land and owed service on it to some of Anglo-Saxon England's great magnates. Azor himself owed allegiance to no less a person than Godwin, the Earl of Wessex, and after him to his son, Harold. Harold was now King Harold II of course, making Azor a king's thegn and giving him a direct line to the royal household, so that he could expect patronage and favours for himself and his family.

On the morning of 28 September 1066 Azor awoke early to busy himself with the affairs of his lands and his household. The day dawned bright and warm for the time of year, and as he looked out over his fields with the harvest gathered and the pigs being driven into the surrounding woodland to forage, all seemed well in Azor's world, and he had no reason to believe that this contented state of affairs would not carry on forever. Even the news from the north of yet another Viking invasion did not trouble the Saxon nobleman, after all York (Eoferwic as he called it, and Jorvik as the Danes knew it) was at the other end of the country.

2. Inscribed near the top of the pillar, one of the earliest dates is 1066 and commemorates the dispossession of the local Anglo-Saxon thegn Azor. Even contemporary Norman records hinted that Azor's land was seized unjustly.

True, Azor had had to send some of his best men to join the King's army over the summer, but they had come home to help with the harvest when no invasion had materialised.

What he did not know was that the anticipated invasion had only been delayed and that very morning only some 50 miles away to the east a great armada was making landfall on Pevensey's long and sandy beach. As the dawn mist was burnt away, any observer on that shore could gaze out over a bay crowded with sleek longships and fat-bottomed transports laden with men, horses and all the supplies necessary for war. Everywhere was bustle as their huge square sail-cloths were being pulled in and stowed by hundreds of seamen. It would seem to that observer that the feared Vikings had indeed come south, but they would have been wrong. True, some of the men coming ashore in mail armour, with swords at their hips and their huge warhorses neighing in the ships' holds, did indeed have Scandinavian blood running through their veins, but these were not northmen but Normans.

Back in Cocking, Azor did not yet know it, but the arrival of these Normans would mean he would be the very last of the line of Cocca to hold sway over the village of his birth. Within the space of a few months, more than 500 years of Saxon history in this beautiful corner of England would come to an end. The invaders landing on Pevensey beach would be like no others the land had seen for centuries and England would never be the same again.

TIMELINE

802	Egbert becomes King of Wessex, he goes on to conquer Mercia and Northumbria and becomes the very first 'Bretwalda' – ruler of all England.
839	Egbert's son Ethelwulf comes to the throne; his reign is plagued by Danish Viking raids and invasions. He defeats the Danes at the Battle of Ockley in Surrey in 851.
866	The Danish 'Great Army' led by the legendary Lothbrokson brothers arrives in East Anglia intent on conquest and settlement and not just raiding. The Army captures York, the capital of the Kingdom of Northumbria.
867	Having lost York to the Northumbrians, the Danes attack the city again and destroy the Northumbrian Saxon army. York – Jorvik – becomes the capital of Viking England.
871	Alfred comes to the throne of Wessex. He will become the only ever English king to be called 'the Great'.
878	Alfred crushes Guthrum's Danish army at the Battle of Edington in Wiltshire.

Timeline

899	Alfred's son, Edward the Elder, comes to the throne and faces growing Danish pressure on his borders. He responds by re-conquering East Anglia and parts of Mercia.
924	Athelstan, Edward's son, succeeds to the throne and decisively defeats an army of Scots and Vikings at Brunanburh in Yorkshire in 937. Olaf Guthfrithson's Vikings and their allies lose five kings and seven of Olaf's earls killed on the battlefield, as well as the son of Constantine II of Scotland.
947	Erik Bloodaxe, the Norwegian Viking leader, is crowned King of Northumbria in York.
954	After having been deposed once and then reinstated, Erik Bloodaxe is finally thrown off the Northumbrian throne by the local citizenry. He will be the last King of Northumbria and York.
978	Edward the Martyr is murdered in Corfe Castle, probably by his brother Ethelred.
991	Ethelred earns the nickname of 'the Unready' meaning 'badly advised' as well as 'ill-prepared'. He makes the disastrous decision to try and buy off the Viking invaders with huge sums of gold and silver, the so-called Danegeld.
1002	Ethelred orders the wholesale massacre of Danish settlers in England on St Brice's Day.
1013	Svein Forkbeard, King of Denmark, invades England. Ethelred and his family flee to Normandy.
1014	Ethelred returns to England to reclaim his throne. An inconclusive war leads to the division of the country into the northern Danelaw and the English south after Ethelred's death.

1016

Ethelred's son, Edmund II 'Ironside', dies the same year he is crowned. The throne passes to the Viking leader, Canute, the son of the Danish king, Svein. Canute brings peace and unites England with Denmark and then Norway into a vast Viking empire and marries Ethelred's widow Emma. During his reign the Saxon-Scandinavian Godwin family from Wessex rises to pre-eminence, the patriarch Earl Godwin, becoming the most powerful man in the country behind the King.

1035

Harthacanute, Canute's son, succeeds but is abroad in Denmark fighting Magnus to retain control of Norway. England splits between Harthacanute and his half-brother Harald Harefoot. William – the illegitimate son of Robert I – becomes Duke of Normandy at the age of seven.

1036

Ethelred's sons, Edward and Alfred, arrive in England where Alfred is murdered by the Danes and Edward forced to flee once more.

1037

Harald Harefoot declared king as Harald I, but dies three years later.

1040

Harthacanute succeeds once more, but his unpopular rule ends with his death in 1042.

1042

Edward again returns from exile and restores the Saxon royal line of Cerdic to the English throne. A pious and scholarly king, Edward 'the Confessor' orders the building of Westminster Abbey.

1047

The combined forces of William, Duke of Normandy and King Henry I of France win the Battle of Val-ès-Dunes against the forces of several rebel Norman barons, led by Gui of Brionne, the son of Reginald I, Count of Burgundy. As a result, William secures his control of the dukedom.

Timeline

Married but with no male heir, the ageing Edward is undecided on the succession.

5 January
Edward I dies. The same day, the *Witangemot*, the council of the most powerful men in the land, elect Harold Godwinson as King Harold II.

April
Halley's comet is visible in the English night sky. William of Poitiers in his *History of William the Conquerer* considered it 'the presage of [Harold's] doom'.

20 September
The English earls and brothers, Edwin of Mercia and Morcar of Northumbria, are routed at the Battle of Fulford, near York, by the Norwegian king, Harald Sigurdsson 'Hardrada' – 'hard ruler', and his English ally Tostig Godwinson, King Harold's own younger brother.

25 September
The Battle of Stamford Bridge. While relaxing in the sunshine around the River Derwent, the Vikings are caught by surprise by King Harold's army and annihilated. Tostig and Hardrada are killed and the Viking threat to England destroyed.

28 September
William and his invasion fleet land at Pevensey beach in Sussex.

14 October
The Battle of Hastings. Fought from around 9am until late afternoon, the English are utterly destroyed. King Harold and his two brothers, Leofwine and Gyrth, are slain, along with large numbers of England's Anglo-Saxon aristocracy and the majority of the country's professional fighting men, the housecarles.

1066

HISTORICAL BACKGROUND

Why was Anglo-Saxon England such a target for foreign invasions in 1066, and why did England's king find himself facing a French army on a hill near Hastings in the late autumn of that year? By 1066 England was one of the wealthiest and most prosperous countries in Europe. It was also disunited and had been in a state of turmoil for more than two and a half centuries. Viking raiders from Scandinavia had overrun most of the north, the midlands and East Anglia, as well as the Orkneys, the Shetlands, parts of Scotland, the western Isles and even large tracts of Ireland. The Anglo-Saxon fightback had been led by the southern kingdom of Wessex and strong rulers such as Alfred and Athelstan. Problems with royal succession were always England's Achilles heel however, and 1066 saw a fatal breakdown in the ruling dynasty that opened up the country to the threat of multiple invasions from rival claimants to the suddenly vacant throne.

Edward I, called The Confessor, died at the beginning of January with no male heir, and having not made it clear who was to succeed him; the result was chaos. The *Witangemot*, England's high council, elected the most prominent noble in the land, Harold Godwinson Earl of Wessex, to the throne. Powerful as he was, Harold did not command the total allegiance of the north of his kingdom, and having no royal blood his claim to the throne was

3. Edward the Confessor, as depicted in the Bayeux Tapestry.

weak. Across the North Sea, the King of Norway, the celebrated warrior Harald Sigurdsson called 'Hardrada' (Hard-ruler), saw an opportunity, and even though he had no blood claim to the throne either, prepared to invade, aided by one of Harold Godwinson's own brothers, Tostig. But Hardrada was not the only foreigner to have his eyes on England, to the south in northern France, lay the duchy of Normandy. Seized by Viking raiders years before, Normandy had evolved into a powerful mini-state bent on military expansion. Its ruler, Duke William, was intent on pressing his claim to the English throne, related as he was, albeit distantly, by marriage to the late King Edward, who almost certainly promised him the throne years previously.

With three rivals for the crown, huge internal instability, and the rich prize of England up for grabs, 1066 was set to be one of the most momentous years in English history.

England in 1066

Across Europe in the eleventh century agriculture was the basis of the economy, and then, as now, England's land was fertile and supported a wealth of crops and livestock. Wheat and barley were the main staples, with an abundance of pigs and sheep in particular – wool was already a major export.

Fish were plentiful too, both fresh and saltwater, and were extensively farmed for food. A single cultivated farmed fishpond in Petersham in Surrey produced an incredible 1000 eels and 1000 lampreys (an exceedingly ugly fish related to the common eel) every year. The country was overwhelmingly rural, with 90 per cent of the population of almost two million living on the land, mostly in small villages like Cocking.

Those same villages produced most things people needed in their daily lives, but there was also trade and markets for goods across the large number of towns and cities spread across the country and linked by the remnants of the old Roman road system.

CULTURED AND CULTIVATED

It is a myth that Anglo-Saxon England was somehow backward and underdeveloped. A full 80 per cent of the farmland in England recorded in the 1914 national survey was already under the plough in 1066. There was a flourishing cultural and artistic tradition in the country, with the monasteries and churches at the heart of it, producing magisterial works of art and literature such as the Lindisfarne Gospels and *Beowulf*.

ROADS

The Romans began to build roads in Britain immediately after their invasion, the primary aim being to facilitate the swift movement of troops around the country to maintain Roman rule. The network was complete by around AD 180. Eventually totalling about 2000 miles, the most important roads linked London (*Lundene*) with the key ports of Dover (*Dubris*), Chichester (*Noviomagus*) and Portchester (*Portus Adurni*); and the main Roman army bases of York (*Eboracum*), base of the Ninth Legion; Chester (*Deva*), base of the Twentieth: and Caerleon (*Isca Augusta*), base of the Second. After the Romans left systematic construction of paved highways did not resume in England until the eighteenth century.

Then, as now, the biggest city in the land was London in the earldom of Mercia, with 15,000–20,000 inhabitants, although the official capital of the kingdom was Winchester (*Wintonceastre*) in Hampshire. This was where the royal court was most often located, although it travelled around almost continuously. Winchester itself was smaller than London, with perhaps 9000 inhabitants, about the same as the unofficial 'capital' of the north, the great Northumbrian city of York. Called *Eoferwic* by the Anglo-Saxons, York had been conquered by the Danes almost two centuries before in 867, re-named Jorvik, and made the capital of Viking England for almost 100 years.

Government administration in Anglo-Saxon England was efficient, with systems for holding land, and the paying of taxes and services related to it. These laws and duties were well understood and adhered to, and the entire legal system itself was pretty advanced after Alfred had had it reformed and codified.

The Anglo-Saxon church was strong, with the Sees of Canterbury and York being the most important in England, and Christianity dominated, although pockets of paganism still held out, especially among the new Scandinavian settlers in the midlands and the north.

POPULATION DECLINE

The population of Roman Britain had been around four million, roughly double what it was at the time of the Norman Conquest. Although Anglo-Saxon England was a comparatively rich country, mortality rates were still incredibly high due to intermittent famine, diseases such as arthritis, leprosy and tuberculosis, and almost constant warfare.

The Vikings in England

Those settlers, and how they had come to live in England, had been the dominating feature of life in Anglo-Saxon England for more than 200 years and would play a crucial role in the events of 1066 and the Battle of Hastings itself. Little is known about Scandinavia – the modern-day countries of Norway, Denmark and Sweden – before their inhabitants burst into history as the marauding 'Vikings' in the late eighth century. It may well be that they first came to England as traders, but whether they did or not they swiftly turned to violence, as they began raiding up and down England's long coastline. The Anglo-Saxon Chronicle's report on the killing of the king's reeve (actually '*shire reeve*' – a royal official whose title was later shortened to 'sheriff') in Portland was the first such documented incident that we know of, but it was the attack on Lindisfarne five years later that put them centre stage in England. After that, flotillas of longships came across the North Sea in search of easy plunder.

Viking incursions of course fell most heavily in the east and north, with the Humber estuary in particular acting as a gateway for the raiders and their dragon-prowed ships. Anglo-Saxon England struggled to adapt to face this new threat. Although occasionally united under a series of kings from the royal house of Wessex, in reality the country was still a patchwork of five separate kingdoms: Wessex, Mercia, Northumbria, East Anglia and Kent.

4. *The Lindisfarne Stone, Northumberland. A late ninth- or tenth-century grave marker showing a procession of Viking warriors.*

CLIMATE CHANGE

The global temperature rose by over one degree centigrade in the centuries after the fall of the Roman Empire in what is known as the 'Little Climatic Optimum'. This led to increases in food production and the flooding of low-lying land, especially in northern Europe, which helped fuel population growth as well as mass migration. This natural phenomenon was a root cause of both the Anglo-Saxon and Viking attacks on the British Isles as surplus people looked for somewhere else to live.

5. King Alfred the Great.

England's rich, but poorly defended, churches and monasteries were the Vikings' primary target at first, but it wasn't long before relatively small-scale raiding was replaced by full-scale expeditions carried out by thousands of men and hundreds of ships. This trend escalated until the late 860s when, for the very first time, a large enough Viking force to warrant the title 'The Great Army', commanded by the Lothbrokson brothers, landed in East Anglia and made it clear it had come to conquer and not merely to loot. Establishing a pattern that would last for the best part of the next two centuries, the Vikings took advantage of the disunity of the Anglo-Saxon kingdoms and began to pick them off one by one.

Firstly, they scared the East Anglian King, Edmund, into buying them off, and then they marched north into Northumbria, right into the middle of a civil war raging between King Osberht and a rival claimant for the throne, Aelle. With the Saxons fighting among themselves, the Great Army captured York and established it as their capital. Next to fall was Mercia in 874, and most of Wessex was then taken in a campaign four years later. Only the inspired kingship of Alfred the Great and his successors; Edward the Elder and Athelstan, stopped Anglo-Saxon England disappearing altogether.

Eventually the country settled on a divide – the so-called *Danelaw*. Northumbria, East Anglia, and the five boroughs of Leicester, Nottingham, Derby, Stamford and Lincoln became Viking lands, while Wessex, Kent and the western half of Mercia stayed English, in effect a 'super-Wessex'. In the new Danelaw, Scandinavians, mainly Danes but also Norwegians, settled in large numbers, and with the border being fairly porous they also drifted south into Anglo-Saxon England and set themselves to farming and trading. Northern England became not so much Anglo-Saxon as Anglo-Viking, with an aristocracy and people that naturally looked across the sea to Scandinavia, so also providing any would-be Viking invader with a ready-made pool of potential supporters.

The Dukedom of Normandy

The Vikings were also progenitors of the other great claimant for the English throne in 1066 – William, Duke of Normandy. Two hundred years before Hastings the northern coast of modern-day France was a favoured area for Viking raids. River estuaries, as in England, provided the Vikings with tailor-made highways deep into the interior, up which they could sail to plunder and loot at will. Just as in England, Viking incursions soon escalated from raiding, to invasion and then finally to settlement. Paris itself was besieged by a Viking army from 885–886, and when that attempt failed one of the Viking leaders led his men west, determined to salvage something from the failure. His name was Rollo (also called *Hrolf*), and nicknamed 'the Ganger' on account of his extremely long legs. Rollo and his men seized a sizeable territory at the mouth of the Orne and Seine estuaries and used it as a base to carry on raiding deep into France. Eventually the French king, Charles the Simple, decided the best way to deal with them was to hand them the rights to the land they occupied in return for support against other Viking bands that were plaguing his kingdom at the time. The result was the creation of what would become the duchy of Normandy – the land of the 'northmen'. Normandy is an area of about 20,000 square miles, roughly the same size as Belgium, with a French population at the time numbering around 500,000. Rollo's men were relatively few, numbering a few thousand at most, so overall the region stayed resolutely French in make-up, particularly as the invaders had come south without any women from their homeland and so ended up marrying local Frenchwomen. It made sense for them to learn the local language too, and within no more than a generation Viking Norman society was overwhelmingly French in complexion. More than a century later, Rollo's direct descendant, Emma of Normandy, married King Ethelred of England, linking the two lands. Meanwhile her brother, Duke Robert I, seduced a beautiful young girl in the town

6. *William Duke of Normandy, in a somewhat romantic Victorian depiction.*

of Falaise, where his castle was situated. She was called Herlève, and was the daughter of a local tanner called Fulbert. The bastard she gave birth to in the autumn of 1028 was christened 'William'.

50 Years of Invasions and Alliances

Meanwhile over in England, the 50 years in the run up to Hastings had seen the country undergo dramatic upheavals. The Danish King Svein Forkbeard invaded in 1013, forcing King Ethelred and his family to seek refuge at his brother-in-laws court in Normandy. Three years later Ethelred returned to England for what turned out to be a truly disastrous year for his family. Unable to eject the Danes from his kingdom, Ethelred had no choice but to accept the reality of the Danelaw, before dying in ignominy.

He was followed to the grave in quick succession by his eldest son, Edmund II called 'Ironside', and one of Edmund's two sons (also called Edmund – the other, Edward, would die in 1057). Another of Ethelred's sons, Eadwig, and a distant cousin Aethekward, were murdered by the Danes as the royal House of Cerdic was decimated.

The resultant power vacuum enabled Svein's son, Canute, to seize the throne and make himself King Canute I of England. To help cement his claim, Canute married Ethelred's widow Emma of Normandy, setting aside his first wife, the Northampton heiress Aelfgifu. Canute then combined England with Denmark and

7. *King Ethelred II 'The Unready'.*

DANEGELD

Following the Viking victory at Maldon in Essex in 991, Ethelred paid the invaders 3300kg of silver to leave. Known at the time as '*gafol*' (tribute) these payments would later become infamous as 'Danegeld'. Ethelred bought two years peace with the Danes for 13,400kg of silver in 1007, then in 1012, following the sack of Canterbury, another 17,900kg of silver was paid. Ethelred was not the only king of England to pay Danegeld; in 1018 Canute paid an army of his fellow Danes 30,800kg of silver, 3900kg of it from London alone. As a result, more Anglo-Saxon silver has been found in Sweden than in England.

Norway (which he also ruled) into a vast northern empire that for two decades was the most powerful state in Europe. Within England he replaced its ancient kingdoms with less-powerful earldoms, presided over by loyal supporters such as Thorkell the Tall in East Anglia, and a number of Anglo-Saxon 'new men' including Siward, made Earl of Northumbria, Leofric Earl of Mercia, and chief among them all, a Sussex *thegn* (a fairly low Anglo-Saxon rank of nobiliy) in his late twenties called Godwin, whom Canute elevated and made Earl of Wessex.

Little is known of Godwin before his promotion, save his father was an ambitious Saxon naval commander called Wulfnoth who had already changed sides and allied himself with the Danes. Godwin was as ambivalent in his loyalty as his father, and also astute enough to marry Gytha, King Canute's Danish sister-in-law. The couple went on to have six sons and two daughters who would grow up to dominate England until Stamford Bridge and Hastings almost wiped out the Godwinson family. England was thus well on its way to becoming a Scandinavian nation with a Danish king, an Anglo-Viking aristocracy, and inter-marriage rife between Saxons and Danes.

8. *A coin of Ethelred II 'The Unready'.*

9. *A coin of Canute.*

However, when Canute died in his forties in Shaftesbury in 1035, this possibility faded as his sons; the half-brothers Harthacanute (son of the Norman Emma) and his elder brother Harald Harefoot (son of the English Aelfgifu) disputed the succession. With the 18-year-old Harthacanute in Denmark, struggling to keep his late father's empire together, Harald remained in England, winning over the allegiance of the nobility, especially Godwin. The dynastic waters were then further muddied when Emma's two other sons by Ethelred; the *Atheling* (Saxon term for heir to the throne) Alfred and his younger brother Edward, landed in England from Normandy, ostensibly to visit their mother in Winchester, but more likely to assess the opportunity to retake the crown. The mission was a disaster. Almost certainly betrayed by Godwin, Alfred was seized in Guildford by Harald's men and his own retainers were slaughtered. Shipped off to the swamp-encircled Isle of Ely in East Anglia, Alfred's eyes were torn out and he died shortly afterwards. Edward fled back to Normandy, lucky to escape with his life.

With the Saxon threat seen off, Harald felt secure enough to have himself crowned Harald I of England. His reign had lasted barely three years when he died in Oxford in March 1040. Harthacanute, meanwhile, had already gathered an invasion fleet in Denmark and lost no time in sailing to England and reclaiming his lost throne. In an act of vengeance for his half-brothers usurpation and his murder of Alfred (Harthacanute's other half-brother), the new king had Harald's body exhumed from its burial site in Westminster, beheaded and thrown into a marsh next to the Thames. Everything now seemed set fair for the 23-year-old Danish monarch, but he proceeded to alienate the English with his high-handed attitude and heavy taxes, so few tears were shed when he died suddenly at a wedding feast in Lambeth two years later. He would be the last true Viking ever to sit on the throne of England, and with his death, Canute's great Scandinavian empire broke up, never to be resurrected.

Of the seventeen children fathered by Ethelred and Canute, only one was now still alive – Ethelred and Emma's son, Edward. Already almost 40 years old, Edward had spent most of his life in exile in Normandy with his mother's people. More Norman French than English, he was nevertheless acceptable to both the Anglo-Saxon and Scandinavian factions in England, and he was declared king in 1042. His reign would last almost a quarter of a century and would be a rare period of relative peace and stability. But by the autumn of 1065, Edward was more than 60 years old, a remarkable feat in itself, and although in many ways a successful king, he had nevertheless failed in his most important function – the provision of an heir. His 20-year marriage to Earl Godwin's daughter, Edith, was childless, and yet again it would be dynastic uncertainty that would prove the trigger for upheaval in England.

10. A coin of Harthacanute.

11. A coin of Edward the Confessor.

Internal strife in Scandinavia had more or less removed the Viking threat during Edward's long reign, and instead he had been plagued by the nobility. By 1051 his father-in-law Godwin and his family had come to dominate the country, controlling Wessex, East Anglia, and the southern half of Mercia. Desperate to counter-balance this potential menace, and mindful of his Norman heritage, Edward had bestowed lands and titles on a small number of Normans; men like Robert fitzWimarc, Ralph of Mantes (whose mother had actually been Edward's sister Godgifu) and Robert of Jumièges, the latter two created the earl of Hereford and Archbishop of Canterbury respectively. Edward also made overtures to Duke William about the possibility of his succession to the English throne. After all, William had a claim through Edward's own mother Emma, whose grandnephew he was, and Edward had known the young duke since his birth. Edward was also very much at home with his continental cousins and their language and culture but this growing Norman influence roused English anger, and when Edward's brother-in-law, Count Eustace II of Boulogne, fell into a fight in Dover with the townsfolk, the scene was set for conflict.

Furious at the Dover attack on Eustace, Edward ordered Godwin to 'harry' Dover and the surrounding countryside. This was a standard punishment and would normally have seen the town burned and the local population either killed or driven from their homes. Godwin refused, summoned his sons and rebelled against his king. By the beginning of September the two armies faced each other near Tetbury in Gloucestershire, and civil war seemed imminent. Cool heads prevailed, and a *Witangemot* was called for later that month in London. The Godwin family decided not to wait, fleeing into exile in Ireland and Flanders. Within a year they were back, and after a series of clashes with Edward's forces, peace was finally made in London in September 1052.

Godwin died the following year, and the mantle of leadership in his family fell to his second son, Harold, his eldest Swein having died on pilgrimage. As Earl of Wessex, Harold became Edward's chief advisor and England's military strongman. With his younger brother Tostig, the Earl of Northumbria, he defeated the Welsh King Gruffydd ap Llywelyn of Gwynedd and Powys in 1062–3, before having to abandon Tostig himself when the Northumbrians rose in revolt against him in 1065. Supported by his elder brother Edwin, the Earl of Mercia, Morcar was installed as Earl of Northumbria, and the House of Leofric now effectively counterbalanced the power of the Godwinsons. The two families then united when Harold married Ealdgyth, Edwin and Morcar's sister.

That winter Edward fell gravely ill, unable even to attend the consecration of his beloved Westminster Abbey on 28 December. He died on 5 January 1066 at the advanced age of 63.

NASTY, BRUTISH AND SHORT

Life expectancy in Anglo-Saxon England was typically to the late 30s or early 40s. Excavation of Anglo-Saxon cemeteries in Hampshire dug up some 65 graves dating from between AD 400 to 1000. Dating of the remains found none had lived past 45, although kings did better, averaging 48 years old when they died, making Edward one of the longest lived men of his time.

That same day, in an unprecedented move, the Witangemot's 60 or so lords and prelates set aside the claim of the fourteen-year-old Atheling Edgar (Edmund Ironside's grandson) and elected the commoner, Harold Godwinson, as King. They were influenced no doubt by Edward's words to Harold on his deathbed: 'I commend this woman [the queen] and all the kingdom to your protection.'

The following day, even as Edward's body was laid to rest in the new Westminster Abbey, King Harold II was crowned. His reign would last less than ten months, during which time he would oppose two foreign invasions, fight two major battles and win a great victory, before it all would end at Hastings. To understand what happened that fateful day it is essential to also understand the battles of Fulford and Stamford Bridge that happened in the weeks before. In an age when major battles were relatively few, the miracle was not that Harold went down to defeat against the Normans, but just how close he came to victory.

12. *The coronation of King Harold II. Archbishop Stigand is shown on his left; he had not journeyed to Rome to receive his archbishopric from the Pope and so was viewed by the papacy as illegitimate. He managed to hang on nevertheless for several years after William's accession, not being replaced until 1070.*

THE ARMIES

By the time of Hastings, war had been endemic throughout Europe for centuries. Peace was rare and fleeting, with anything from low-level raiding for slaves and plunder, up to full-scale invasions and seizures of power, commonplace. This brutal landscape was founded on the traditional right of every freeman to bear arms, and although these rights were still in place in 1066, societies across Western Europe were evolving more sophisticated structures within which to conduct warfare. None of the hosts that faced each other in 1066, either at Fulford, Stamford Bridge or Hastings, were what we would call today a professional standing army, but they were beginning to look like them, with the majority of the men who would fight in 1066 no longer being freebooting warriors but professional soldiers. They were recruited, equipped, trained and paid by their lord to whom they owed service unto death, and increasingly that lord was a king, or in Normandy's case a duke. Those lords were multi-skilled, being politicians, landowners and judges, however by far their most important role was still as military commander. Unlike their men they underwent no formal training but relied instead on the experience they had gained throughout their lifetime.

Then, as now, war was both expensive and international. A man's kit and equipment depended on the contents of his lord's purse. Many of those men and commanders would have fought abroad and have an understanding of the tactics of other armies and their campaigning styles. They were the products of efficient military systems, capable of raising relatively large numbers of seasoned soldiers, and the money and supplies needed to maintain them in the field. None of the armies that fought that autumn was less than about 6000 men strong, and Anglo-Saxon England managed to field no less than three such armies in a matter of weeks. Overall this meant that across the battlefields of England in 1066 the men who fought each other so savagely would be similarly equipped and trained, would almost all have significant combat experience, would have experienced leaders, and would know what to expect from their enemies in terms of tactics.

The Commanders

William Duke of Normandy

William, (*Guillaume*) was 39 years old when he invaded England. A man of huge experience and iron will, he was one of the most gifted commanders of his age and a formidable opponent. At just under six feet tall he was quite a bit above the average height, and years of training and combat had made him physically very strong. Nicknamed '*rufus*' as a child he may have had red hair, although it was probably more likely this referred to his ruddy complexion. His own son, also called William, would earn the same sobriquet. Although often shown in idealised portraits with a moustache, he may well have been clean-shaven with close-cropped hair, given that this was the fashion at the time amongst the Norman aristocracy. He was illiterate, relying for his letters on his advisers and scribes, most of whom were educated churchmen. Although a direct descendant of Rollo, and hence Scandinavian by blood, his mother tongue was Norman French and he never learned English, never seeing the need, as under his rule French would take over as the language of English government after the Conquest.

13. William the Conqueror, as depicted in a modern statue at his birthplace at Falaise, Normandy.

As his father Duke Robert's only son, even an illegitimate one, William succeeded to the duchy at the tender age of seven when his father died on pilgrimage to Jerusalem in 1035. For the next decade the child-duke lived in constant danger from those seeking to overthrow him, many of them his own relatives. His steward Osbern, and two of his guardians were murdered trying to protect him, and on one occasion, in the castle of Vaudreuil, he only survived due to a case of mistaken identity when the assassin sent to kill him stabbed to death the child in the bed next to the sleeping William. It was only when he allied himself with King Henry I of France and defeated a rebel army, led by his cousin Gui of Brionne, at the Battle of Val-ès-Dunes in 1047 that he finally secured his rule. Having survived his turbulent minority, the young and charismatic duke then proceeded to grow his power by

14. Falaise, the birthplace of William the Conqueror. The towers were built after his death.

military force and diplomatic guile. Surrounded by powerful rivals he began by securing the support of the County of Flanders to the north by marrying the Flemish heiress Matilda, despite the Pope's objections. The next-door dukedom of Brittany was next, and was subdued by military force after a series of border skirmishes followed by invasion. To the south of Normandy lay Maine, a prize which drew William into conflict with Geoffrey Martell's Anjou. It was only after Martell's death that William secured the area as part of his own fiefdom. William's ambition even set him against his former patron, Henry I of France, and the two men fought inconclusive campaigns against each other in 1054 and 1057.

By the 1060s William was in his prime. He had been fighting almost continuously for more than two decades, and was recognised as general of rare talent. Warfare was not his only gift

15. The fortress of Caen in western Normandy, a stronghold of Duke William.

though, he was also well versed in the intricacies of diplomacy and the forging of alliances, and his abilities in this field would be one of the deciding factors at Hastings. In 1066 William was able to leave Normandy unguarded and take every man with a sword with him to England, as his borders were kept safe by watchful neighbours, who also contributed men to the Norman army. Indeed, over a third of William's force at Hastings was composed of non-Norman allies, and they marched under a papal banner of support bestowed on them by Rome, mollified after William and Matilda's marriage by the building and gifting of rich cathedrals and monasteries to the Church. By contrast, Harold would stand alone at Hastings, shorn of any support, even from his own northern earls.

William centralised government within Normandy, reforming the administration and creating a new aristocracy that owed its position and fortune to him and him alone. This relatively small group of men, called his 'Companions', would be his key subordinates

HOSTAGES

It was customary at the time for important hostages to be exchanged between houses and countries. Harold's own youngest brother, Wulfnoth, born around 1045, had been sent along with Swein Godwinson's son Hakon, to Normandy on Edward's orders at the time of the Godwinson's rebellion. Harold saw him in Rouen for the first time in over ten years, and was allowed by William to take Hakon home when he left, but Wulfnoth would remain a hostage until William's death in 1087.

during the invasion of England. The two most important were his half-brothers Odo and Robert, both sons of the nobleman Herluin de Conteville whom Duke Robert had married to William's mother Herlève following William's own birth. Odo was nine years William's junior, headstrong and tempestuous, despite being the bishop of Bayeux. His own full brother, Robert, was a year or two younger than Odo and had been created Count of Mortain.

Alongside them were Eustace II Count of Boulogne (the same Eustace whose fracas in Dover had ignited the Godwinson's revolt against Edward and was known as '*aux Gernons*' – 'with moustaches'), Walter Giffard, Lord of Longueville, Richard FitzGilbert who was married to Giffard's daughter Rohese, William Count of Evreux, Roger de Beaumont, Geoffrey de Mortagne, William fitz Osbern, Aimeri, Viscount of Thouars, Hugh, Lord of Montfort-sur-Risle, Ralph de Tosny, Lord of Conches, Hugh de Grandmesnil, William de Warenne, William Malet, Turstin fitz Rolf and Engenulf de Laigle. These men were experienced soldiers who had served in William's wars and grown rich and powerful under his patronage, and each commanded large numbers of well armed troops who would form the backbone of the Norman army at Hastings.

16. *The Bayeux Tapestry was made in Canterbury, probably on the orders of William's half-brother Odo. This particular piece purports to show Harold Godwinson swearing on sacred relics he would support William's claim to the English throne.*

The army they would defeat would be commanded by a commoner made king – Harold II Godwinson, a man William knew well. They first met in 1064 when Harold, as the Earl of Wessex and the country's pre-eminent noble, was sent to France on a diplomatic mission, perhaps on King Edward's orders to affirm his future allegiance to William as Edward's chosen successor. Landing in Ponthieu, by mistake he was taken captive by the local count, a vassal of the Norman duke. William swiftly obtained Harold's release and entertained him at his court in Rouen before taking him with him on his decisive expedition against neighboring Brittany.

Harold was given a command in William's army, and distinguished himself both in battle and by saving the lives of two Norman knights who almost drowned in quicksand. Harold was with William when his long-time nemesis Conan II, the aged Duke of Brittany, finally surrendered at his castle of Dinan, and it was at this time that Harold supposedly offered William his support for his claim to the throne, and made oaths to that effect, including swearing on sacred relics, if the Bayeux Tapestry is to be believed.

Whether he did or not, it was clear that William felt Harold had promised him his allegiance, and the Duke was filled with rage when he heard of Harold's coronation. William felt cheated, and was determined to invade and take the crown he saw as his by right, by force.

King Harold II of England

William's opponent was Harold Godwinson, King Harold II of England, a man who has gone down in history as a brave but doomed loser, famous for being killed at Hastings by an arrow

17. The statue of King Harold II Godwinson at Waltham Abbey. Often described as England's last Anglo-Saxon monarch, Harold was actually half-Danish through his mother Gytha, and is better described as the last king of Anglo-Viking England.

through his eye. Whilst we cannot be certain whether he was killed by that legendary arrow, we do know a lot about the man himself. Like William, Harold was about six feet tall and very strong, many tales of his youth speak of his physical prowess. He was older than William by about five years, although we are not entirely sure as to his exact birth year, putting him well into middle age by the time he came to the throne. He was blond-haired and blue-eyed, and it was likely he had a moustache and perhaps a beard, given that both were customary amongst the English nobility of the time. His looks were an inheritance from his mixed Saxon and Danish ancestry, and although he is forever cast as the last Anglo-Saxon king of England, in reality he was Anglo-Viking, and as such he duly represented the great majority of England's aristocracy, which by this time was a thorough mix of Scandinavian and Anglo-Saxon blood.

It is difficult to get an unbiased picture of Harold's character as so much that was written about him was coloured by the politics of the authors themselves. Chroniclers Orderic Vitalis and William of Poitiers, for instance, were writing after Hastings and were clearly not going to defy the new king and lament Harold's passing. What we do know though is that he was personally courageous, and an experienced military commander, indeed one of the finest of his day. In 1062–3 as the Earl of Wessex, he and his younger brother Tostig, Earl of Northumbria, launched a lightning campaign into Wales to destroy Gruffydd ap Llywelyn, King of Gwynedd and Powys, and break the dangerous alliance between Gruffydd and the earls of Mercia that was threatening much of England. The campaign was a resounding success, with Harold adapting to local conditions and transforming the way his men fought. Out went road-bound heavy infantry and the shield wall, and in came flying columns of lightly armed men taking on the native Welsh in their own hills and mountains. The result was the destruction of Gruffydd's army and the subjugation of Wales to the English crown.

Just like William though, warfare was not Harold's only talent, and his early career demonstrated a gift for diplomacy and politicking that mirrored William's own successes. Still not a united country by Edward's death, England was dominated by its three great earldoms of Northumbria, Mercia and Wessex, which continued to maintain an enormous amount of independence. Harold, as Godwin's second son, inherited his father's earldom of Wessex on his troublesome elder brother Swein's death while on pilgrimage to Jerusalem, and Wessex would be Harold's power-base until his death. Both Mercia and Northumbria ended up being held by a rival to the Godwins, the House of Leofric. Originally created Earl of Mercia by Canute, Leofric had been succeeded by his son Aelfgar who had competed with the Godwins for years. On his own death in 1062, Aelfgar's fourteen-year-old son Edwin inherited Mercia, while his younger brother Morcar (also spelt 'Morkere') would become Earl of Northumbria. Canute's appointment as his premier noble in the north had been the Saxon nobleman Siward, but his house had not prospered and his heir had been killed in an expedition against the Scottish king Macbeth in 1054. A year later, when Siward died, his earldom had been granted by Edward to Harold's 30-year-old younger brother Tostig. The Queen's favourite, Tostig was at first welcomed in the north, but within a decade he had alienated his Anglo-Scandinavian subjects by imposing heavy taxes and favouring his southern friends over the local nobility, several of whom he had murdered while under a supposed flag of truce. The result was rebellion, as recorded by the Anglo-Saxon Chronicle. 'All the men of his earldom were unanimous in repudiating him, and outlawed him and all those with him who had promoted injustice, because he robbed God first, and then despoiled of life and land all those over whom he could tyrannise.'

The north rose as one, butchered Tostig's housecarles, ransacked his treasury and marched south to join with their Mercian brethren. '...they slew all his retainers whom they could catch, whether English or Dane, and seized his stock of weapons in York, his gold and silver and all his treasures which they came to hear of anywhere there.'

The rebels offered the earldom to the sixteen-year-old Morcar who accepted it, and joined with his brother in demanding Tostig's

EALDGYTH

Aelfgar's daughter Ealdgyth was a political pawn used by her father and brothers to further their own power and influence. She was initially married to the Welsh king Gruffydd ap Llywelyn to seal the alliance between Mercia and Gwynedd and Powys, before his defeat by Harold, who was presented with the murdered king's head on a platter as proof of his death. This did not stop her from marrying Harold and bearing him two children; Ulf and Harold, the latter born after his father's death. After Hastings the family was captured in Chester and Ulf was held hostage by William until his demise in 1087. Ealdgyth ended up in exile in Dublin, while Harold fled to Norway.

banishment. The country teetered on the brink of civil war, and it was Harold who averted it by refusing to side with his errant brother, instead advising the king to confirm Morcar as Northumbria's new earl. By doing so he earned Tostig's ire, a hatred that would only end with the deposed earl's death at Stamford Bridge. Harold burnished his political credentials still further after assuming the throne by marrying Ealdgyth, sister to Edwin and Morcar. This marriage tied the Houses of Godwin and Leofric together and cemented Harold's position, although it did not stop the two brothers from acting without circumspection against Harald Hardrada and losing the bulk of the army of the north at Fulford.

Tostig was now in open revolt, the loyalty of Edwin and Morcar was suspect, but Harold could rely on two of his other brothers, Gyrth and Leofwine. Gyrth was the Earl of Anglo-Scandinavian East Anglia, while Leofwine's earldom comprised Essex, Middlesex, Bedfordshire, Hertfordshire, Buckinghamshire, Surrey and the old kingdom of Kent. Both were experienced soldiers in their thirties, and commanded large numbers of housecarles. Their support almost enabled Harold to hold out at Hastings.

As opponents Harold and William were fairly evenly matched. Both were vastly experienced soldiers with impressive victories behind them, both also had diplomatic and political talents that marked them out as impressive rulers. However, William had three hugely important advantages over his Anglo-Viking enemy; the first was the unity of his own nobility. After years of rebellions and uprisings William had ruthlessly crushed all internal opposition to his rule and installed a generation of men who were steadfastly loyal to him and him alone, while Harold had a kingdom of which fully two-thirds was in the hands of a rival house and even one of his own brothers was in open revolt against him. Secondly, William's use of diplomacy as a weapon was a cut above Harold's. So much so that not only did the invasion have the blessing and sanction of the Pope, but also William was buttressed by thousands of allied troops from all across France and the Low Countries. These men would play a key role in his victory.

Harald 'Hardrada' Sigurdsson King of Norway

Last but by no means least, William had one more advantage that would prove decisive – a giant who stood well over six feet tall and whose reputation was feared across Europe – Harald Hardrada Sigurdsson. Born in 1015, Hardrada was an old man of 51 by the time he invaded England. He had begun his military career at the Battle of Stilkastad, when as a fifteen-year-old youth he had seen his half-brother, the Norwegian king Olaf the Stout, slain alongside several thousand of his men by Canute of Denmark's vastly larger army. The young Harald then went into an exile that lasted for fifteen years, during which time he wove a legend as the last and greatest of all the Vikings. Accompanied by a handful of survivors from Stilkastad, Harald sailed southeast to the lands of the Scandinavian Rus. There he was gainfully employed as a mercenary by Jaroslav the Wise, a descendant of the legendary Rurik. Harald and his men fought for Jaroslav for several years across modern-day Poland, Estonia and northern Russia; until the lure of fortune took Harald farther south to the city the Vikings called *Miklagard*, literally 'The Great City' – Constantinople. There he joined the Varangian Guard, the Byzantine Emperor's personal bodyguard composed solely of Scandinavian mercenaries. An élite force in the Empire's army, Harald and the Varangians then fought in Bulgaria, the eastern Mediterranean, Sicily and southern Italy, before returning to Constantinople in triumph. But the imperial court was a hotbed of intrigue and cruelty, and Harald was caught up in a revolt against the Emperor Michael V who was ritually blinded on his own wife's orders to render him unfit to rule. During the subsequent factional in-fighting, Harald was thrown in jail, and on his release he and his companions decided enough was enough and headed north back to Jaroslav's court. Loaded with plunder from the Mediterranean campaigns, Harald married Jaroslav's daughter Ellisif, and then headed farther north, back to Scandinavia.

Back home, his nemesis Canute was dead as were his sons Harthacanute and Harald Harefoot, and his teenage nephew Magnus the Good was King of Norway. Temporarily allying with the new Danish king Svein Esfrithson (the man Ellisif would marry after Harald's death at Stamford Bridge); Harald soon switched sides and became Norway's joint ruler with Magnus, until the latter's death in 1047 while fighting the Danes. Harald would continue the war for the best part of the next 20 years until Edward's death in 1066 opened up the possibility of seizing England. Always an opportunist, Harald saw England's disputed succession as the path upon which he would walk to the English throne. He was encouraged in this by none other than Tostig, who after a feeble attempt at stirring up revolt in England had sailed to Norway in the hope of persuading the legendary 'Thunderbolt of the North' into launching an invasion. The Norwegian king's reaction was to summon a fleet and sail for England, and due to the vagaries of the wind it would be Harald's army who would land in England first, not William's.

The Soldiers

The Franco-Norman army that faced Harold at Hastings was not composed of conscripted farmers armed with little more than a wood-axe and dressed in their everyday work clothes, but instead was entirely made up of experienced, professional soldiers. Normandy, just as elsewhere in France, had a mass call-up system to defend the dukedom in times of invasion and general war. This *arrière ban* was not used by William for the conquest since the terms of service did not include accompanying the duke overseas, plus the duke had been forced to build a fleet almost from scratch to transport his forces across the Channel and there was no room to take untrained amateurs. Every place in every ship was precious to William and had been filled with the very best men available to him, the majority of whom owed personal allegiance either to William himself or one of his nobles. As such they had been specially recruited, expensively equipped and rigorously trained for a life of military service.

There were three main types of soldiers; archers, infanteers and cavalrymen. We do not know the exact numbers of each, but we do know that there were probably around 2500 cavalry, with about 3500 infantrymen and 1000 archers. Having the lowest social standing, the bowmen would have been drawn from the peasantry, with most learning to use a bow as they hunted in Normandy's woods and forests. Formal training for them would have been rare, in contrast to the infantry who, though again being of peasant stock, underwent lengthy and comprehensive training to ensure they could use their weapons effectively and operate with their comrades in distinct units. The cavalry were even more rigorously schooled. Mounted fighting was an extremely technical business and required hundreds of hours of dedicated labour to master. These men were the Norman élite. They were heavily armoured and were beginning to use the French term '*chevalier*' to describe themselves, although the old Latin word '*milites*' was probably more common. Warfare in western Europe was beginning to enter a new age, with the long domination of the foot soldier being supplanted by the era of the mounted man, and it would be the Normans who would spearhead this revolution with their heavy cavalry coming to reign supreme throughout Europe and even into the Middle East. Some of those cavalrymen would have been peasants like their infantry brethren but the majority had some level of wealth and many were landholders, albeit on a small scale. Just as with the infantry, the cavalry were not trained to fight en masse but in separate units commanded by their lord. How many were in each unit depended on the lord's wealth and the level of service he owed to the duke. In simple terms, the more land a man owned the more soldiers he was expected to provide, with that number written down and scrupulously adhered to. Odo for instance, owed the service of 120 milites to his half-brother, while a lesser noble like Robert de Cureio owed that of 33. All the men were housed and fed at their lord's expense and were also paid by him, although it was also common for mercenaries to be hired to fill the ranks too. Northern France was full of rootless, landless men, willing to sell their sword to the highest bidder, and large numbers of these men flocked to William's army on hearing his promises of land, gold and booty in England.

The soldiers of Harold's army were quite different from their Norman counterparts. Roughly equal in overall numbers to their enemy, this masked a stark contrast in composition, with the Anglo-Saxon troops being almost entirely made up of infantrymen, with no cavalry and only a handful of archers. The Bayeux Tapestry makes a point of this by only having a single depiction of an English archer at the battle itself. The English did use bowmen; indeed they would play a not insignificant role at Stamford Bridge, but it seems that they were more numerous in the north of the country so Harold had access to very few of them when he raised men in the south to fight at Hastings. The same was true of cavalry in that the English did use them and again they played an important role at Stamford Bridge, but although almost all of Harold's army at Hastings arrived at the battlefield mounted, they then dismounted to fight as infantry. That self-same infantry was made up of three distinct types, of whom the core, the men who would triumph at Stamford Bridge and so nearly win at Hastings, were England's famed *housecarles*.

The housecarles had begun life as a lord's personal bodyguard, and had evolved over time to take on a raft of duties, such as collecting his taxes, helping administer justice and maintaining law and order, as well as performing their main role of acting as his household troops. Almost exclusively from relatively poor backgrounds, a proportion would have been the sons of soldiers, with military service running in the family. They would have been taken into the service of a lord in their early to mid-teens and as a housecarle-to-be would begin a life of dedication to their master and their profession as a soldier. Given a sleeping place in a barrack room next to their lord's hall, they would rise early and start work, a major part of which consisted of hours of weapon and formation training. Operating in units of 10–40 men, they would practise endlessly with spear, sword and shield, forming shield walls, advancing and retreating to order. Training was hard, brutal and never ending, but succeeded in producing a fighting man recognised throughout Europe as amongst the very best. Extremely disciplined and steadfast, it was the housecarles who would form the heart of the shield wall and at Hastings would form the cliff upon which the Norman waves would break. Unfortunately for Harold though, the housecarles were few, and each of England's great magnates would only be able to afford to maintain a relatively small number of them. Hastings would be their curtain call. Never numbering more than perhaps 3000–4000 at most throughout the whole country, almost all of Edwin and Morcar's Mercian and Northumbrian carles would die at Fulford and Stamford Bridge, leaving around 2000 to perish with their king, fulfilling their oaths not to leave the field upon which their lord lay dead.

While the housecarles were the hardwood of Harold's army, they were ably supported by elements of the traditional Anglo-Saxon

18. An Anglo-Saxon housecarle.

MYSTERY BARRACKS

Many historians believe that England's famed royal housecarles were stationed in two bases – one in the south at Wallingford on the Thames, and one near York at a place called 'Slessvik'. These bases were meant to be purpose-built barracks, perhaps modelled on the Danish Trelleborg fortress. Edward the Confessor did indeed hold 15 acres of land at Wallingford which he used to support a handful of housecarles, but Slessvik is a mystery. No archaeological evidence has been found to back up its existence, and it is extremely unlikely that the housecarles were based in any numbers at either location.

citizen's militia, the *fyrd*. Originally the same concept as the French arrière ban in terms of mass call-up, the fyrd had gradually altered over time to produce smaller numbers of far better equipped and trained men called the 'select fyrd'. These men were almost all minor landowners, many of them held the catch-all noble rank of thegn, and they spent large amounts of their time in a military role. It was the select fyrd men of the south who would fight and die with Harold at Hastings, and there were perhaps as many as 3000 of them there. They were not of the premier quality of the housecarles, either in kit, training or experience, but neither were they a rabble as popular stories of the battle suggest. The remainder of the English army was made up of a special kind of mercenary called *lithsmen*. These lithsmen were mostly Danish, and were very much the freebooting war bands of Viking times. Able to fight on land or sea, these adventurers hired themselves out, not as individuals, but as units, complete with their own commanders. They were experienced, and though not as reliable as housecarles, were trustworthy and at least as militarily competent as the select fyrd alongside whom they would serve.

Last but by no means least there were the Norwegians, who although not at Hastings itself, by their actions played a pivotal

NORSE SETTLEMENTS

While the Danes settled in England, the Norse had founded colonies on the 170 islands of the Orkneys and Shetlands, the Isle of Man, the Hebrides, Scotland and even Ireland – Dublin, Limerick, Waterford and Wexford were Viking cities. The Norse spread far but thinly, with overall settler numbers low; Shetland and Orkney held less than 20,000 people each, and no more than 10,000 Norse lived among Ireland's 300,000 inhabitants. Their genetic legacy though is strong, with the populations of the Orkneys and Shetlands having the highest concentration of Norse DNA anywhere in the world outside of Norway itself.

role in the outcome of the battle. To a great extent Harald Hardrada's army was very much a traditional Viking one, and in many ways was composed of much the same sort of soldiers as Harold Godwinson's Anglo-Scandinavian force. There were archers and cavalry, but only in small numbers, with the vast majority of men being infanteers. The Norwegians had their own housecarles, called *huskarlar*, which were pretty much indistinguishable from their English brethren, indeed there is strong evidence to suggest that the idea of the housecarle originated in Scandinavia, and these men formed the core of Hardrada's host. Alongside them were members of the *leidang*, the Norwegian version of the fyrd and the Norman French arrière ban. Much as with the Anglo-Saxon select fyrd, this was no mass call-up for national defence, but the recruitment of several thousand trained men who would follow their king as part of their feudal duties and obligations. They were joined by their own version of lithsmen, bands of the self-same Scandinavian mercenaries who decided to hire themselves out to Norway instead of England, no doubt in the hope of a Norwegian victory and the easy plunder that would follow.

Harald's army was big, perhaps almost 10,000 men strong, and the bulk of them would have been members of the leidang or lithsmen. Assembling such a sizeable host was no mean feat, especially given the need to leave a large enough force behind at home to combat any opportunist attack by Svein Esfrithson's Denmark. Harald's answer was to empty the Norse colonies of the British Isles of men. After crossing the North Sea, he first put into the Orkneys and then Scotland, where he was joined by perhaps as many as 2000 or more Vikings from those lands as well as from the Hebrides, Shetland, and even Ireland.

The Kit

The men who faced each other at Hastings were amongst the best equipped in Europe at the time. Their arms and armour were practical, well-made and costly. There was no such thing as uniforms, but one of the striking features of the battle would have been how similar the armies would have looked. Each man would have been kitted out with leggings and boots, a shirt and headgear, and be armed with at least a shield and spear. In terms of protection, across both armies the majority of men had a helmet, the most common one known as a *spangenhelm*, being rounded to the head, consisting of either a single piece of moulded iron with a nose-guard down the front, or four iron arches with beaten iron strips between. The Scandinavians also favoured the 'spectacle' helmet that provided some protection for the eyes. Those who could not afford a helmet, such as archers, would have worn some sort of cap, most likely one of baked leather perhaps reinforced with iron strips for added protection.

There were two main designs of shield at the battle: the Viking round shield, and the newer kite model favoured by the Norman cavalrymen and Anglo-Saxon housecarles in particular. The traditional round shield of the English shield wall was made from two or three layers of wood laid cross-grained for strength, faced with a covering, sometimes ox-hide. The average size was about 60cm wide and 20mm thick, with the centre being an iron boss riveted on the shield on the outside, protecting an iron grip on the inside for the bearer. It was strong, not overly heavy, and gave its owner useful protection while not restricting his mobility. However, the tendency towards heavier body armour reduced mobility anyway, and to help protect legs in particular the longer and heavier kite shield was increasingly used. Made from linden wood, the kite shield was around 1.25 metres long and 15mm thick, and usually faced with leather reinforced with metal strips. At its top it was about 55cm wide, tapering downwards to a point, and the warrior held it either by means of an adjustable strap round the neck (called a *guige*) in the case of a cavalryman, or by two straps (*enarmes*) in the back of the shield near the top for an infantryman. Shields were occasionally painted in their lords' colour, and sometimes decorated with his emblem, but this practice was dying out.

The main form of protective equipment at Hastings was also the most expensive – the hauberk. Called the *byjarna* by the Scandinavians this was a mail-shirt made up of thousands of tiny iron links interwoven with each other and individually sewn onto a thick leather shirt. Although not proof against a direct spear thrust or sword blow, a hauberk did protect its wearer from glancing blows, and against all but the most powerful arrow and sling hits. The Scandinavian style popular until the beginning of the eleventh century was for a short, relatively light mailcoat reaching to the waist and affording its wearer a lot of agility, but by Hastings this type had largely been overtaken within the élite housecarle and cavalry arms by far longer and heavier hauberks reaching to the knees. They reached to the elbows on the arms, had hoods to protect the neck and fit under the helmet, and were split down the centre between the legs to allow the wearer to ride a horse. For those without the security of a precious hauberk, a padded leather jerkin was about as good as it got.

The main weapon for soldiers of all ranks was the spear. There were two types; light throwing spears akin to javelins, and longer, heavier ones designed for thrusting. Throwing spears were

19. *This fascinating section of the Bayeux Tapestry clearly shows mail hauberks being loaded by servants onto the waiting ships ready to take them across the Channel. Their considerable weight means they are a two-man lift.*

shorter, being 1–1.5m long, with thrusting spears around two metres in length. The blades were usually leaf-shaped with a rib running down the centre, and were fastened to the shaft using a split socket and rivet. The Norman cavalry sometimes used their spears couched underarm, but the majority of illustrations and descriptions picture them using their spears overhand as missiles.

The other main weapon, beside the spear, was the sword. An expensive weapon, handmade by a blacksmith artisan; possession of one denoted status and wealth. Again, as with most arms and armour, all three armies involved in 1066 used the same sort of sword. Usually about 70–80cm long, the blade was wide, around 55mm, with both edges sharpened and the point being slightly rounded – it was a slashing and hacking weapon. A shallow

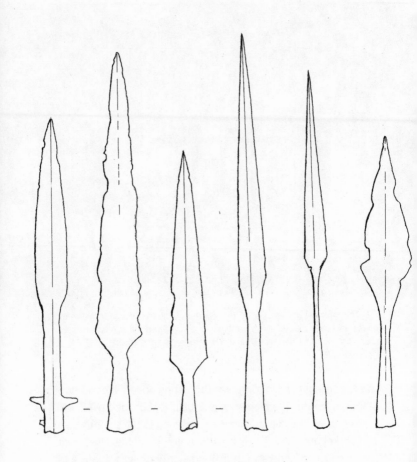

20. Tenth- and eleventh-century English spearheads.

groove, the *fuller*, ran down the centre to reduce weight without lessening strength, but even so the sword weighed in at nearly a kilo. The hilt had a cross-guard usually curved towards the blade, with a grip of wood or bone, bound with anything from simple cloth, to leather or even silver wire. Pommels were large and heavy to counter-balance the blade, and were of the brazil nut or tea-cosy types, so-called because of their appearance. The English and the Scandinavians also carried long knives – the famous *seax* or *scramasax*, the use of which gave the Saxons their name. Around 20cm in length it was a broad-bladed stabbing weapon, with no guard and carried in a simple leather sheath. Archers were equipped with the 'Danish bow' favoured by the Scandinavians, a single piece of wood, usually yew, about 150 to 180cm long and designed to be drawn back to the chest. Effective up to 50 metres or so, it was no Agincourt longbow, but it would prove its worth at Hastings against the densely packed English ranks. The English were also armed with a weapon that inspired dread among the Normans and wreaked havoc at Hastings – the battleaxe. A Viking weapon by origin, it was not universally used by the housecarles, but enough of them were used to cause all the chroniclers to remark on them. The haft was well over a metre in length, with the blades coming in two types; the more traditional bearded axe, called the *skeggox*, was a single-handed weapon with a fairly light blade, straight at the top and curving downwards. These axes could be thrown as well. The other was the truly fearsome broad-axe, with a huge convex blade almost 30cm long from point to point, its weight and power being such that it could literally cleave a mailed man in two. There was no defence against it, but it was nowhere near as prevalent as some historians have believed and was no 'wonder weapon' for Harold.

Similar as most of the arms and armour were at Hastings for both sides, the Normans possessed a truly battle-winning weapon that the English did not – horses. The English did fight from horseback, as did the Scandinavians, but it was the exception and not the rule. For Harold and his men horses were essentially transport, and their tradition was to dismount to fight. Being anything from powerful thoroughbreds down to hill ponies, their main purpose was to carry their rider to a safe location near the chosen battlefield where they would be left in the care of servants while their masters took up position as infantrymen. Across the Channel, the Viking Norman aristocracy had abandoned the infantry shield wall and adopted the Frankish reliance on heavy cavalry as the key to their military prowess. Amongst Normandy's rich pastures, horses were specially bred and trained over generations to produce a warhorse par excellence. Stallions were preferred as mounts rather than mares, with size, speed, discipline and aggression being paramount. They were quick and strong, being able to carry the full weight of a mounted knight, and trained to play their part in battle as they stamped, bit and butted alongside their rider. A Norman cavalryman would spend several hours each day training with his horse so that the two could fight as an effective unit. Their importance to the success of the invasion cannot be overstated, and William knew it. His very risky, and costly, decision to transport well over 2000 of them in the fleet over to England being one of many inspired choices the Norman duke made that autumn. Their presence would dictate the way the battle would be fought and would greatly affect the outcome.

The Tactics

War was, and still is, a vastly expensive and risky pursuit, and in the eleventh century the nature of warfare itself was hugely influenced by economic factors, which largely dictated that hostilities were usually relatively small-scale affairs, where combat was either 'local' – be it a raid or ambush – or occasionally 'regional', cross-border expedition or rebellion, with battles between large opposing armies being rare indeed. That Anglo-Saxon England saw three such battles in the space of a single month in 1066 was a unique historical event, and in all of them the tactics employed were decisive. Hardrada's skilful use of the tried and trusted technique of luring Edwin and Morcar into over-extending themselves at Fulford shattered the northern English army, while the Norwegian was out-thought, as well as out-fought, just days later at Stamford Bridge by the English king. Similarly, it would be William's tactical genius that would prove the difference at Hastings. The tactics employed by the opposing armies were also one of the great mysteries of Hastings. Harold Godwinson was an experienced commander who had shown great tactical innovation throughout his career; the switch to light infantry flying columns against the Welsh and the use of both cavalry and archers against Hardrada's Norwegians being striking examples of immense tactical skill. At Hastings he would lead a well trained and well equipped force that was a match for any in Europe, and yet on the most important battlefield of his life he apparently reverted to nothing more sophisticated than the age-old defensive shield wall. Having carried out two brilliantly successful lightning forced marches from London to York and back – albeit a 'march' on horseback – that defied all military logic, the king of England chose a suitable ridgeline for a defensive position, tethered his horse in the rear alongside his men's and then seemingly stopped making any decisions. Not so his opponent. William never stopped making decisions that fateful day, and the result was his resounding victory. At his disposal he led a force that was a balance of cavalry, infantry and archers, in what was for the time a truly all-arms force. From the outset he would use them as such, and when a tactic did not work he was not afraid to abandon it and try something else, so an initial infantry advance would be replaced by a cavalry charge, to be replaced by rolling cavalry attacks, to then be changed to a combined attack covered by showers of arrows fired by up to 1000 archers. William would seize the initiative at Hastings and never let it go.

Overall, the armies who faced each other in 1066 at Fulford, Stamford Bridge and ultimately at Hastings, had an awful lot in common with each other. They were not composed of untrained amateurs, but of well drilled, well equipped soldiers who were among the very best in Europe at the time. They were broadly the same size, their armour and weapons were similar, and they would have known each other's tactics and fighting styles. After all, the Scandinavians and Anglo-Saxons had been fighting each other for hundreds of years, and the Anglo-Saxons had also been involved in Continental warfare for decades, Harold himself had taken part in William's Brittany campaign of course. They were all composed, in essence, of the same 'types' of men too. The commanders at all levels were almost exclusively members of the nobility. Some, such as the Norman Count Robert de Mortain, the Saxon Earl Leofwine and the Orcadian Norse Jarl Erlend, were great magnates with vast estates and huge retinues, but the majority were minor nobles like the Saxon thegns who would typically bring 30–40 men to the army.

For all these men, war, and training for war, was an integral part of their lives. From an early age they would be schooled in weapon handling and the tactics they were expected to use in combat. The men they led had much in common too. The rank and file were freemen, mostly the sons of farmers and village artisans, and they would have volunteered to become professional warriors when they were little more than children. Their role in their master's household was far more than soldiering, and the title 'retainer' is probably more akin to the way they lived. Fed, clothed and housed by their lord, they were expensive and needed to deliver a return on investment beyond fighting in battles that were, the year 1066 being an extraordinary exception, rare. They would act as tax collectors, land stewards, messengers, and labourers when required, basically whatever was needed at the time. They were young, typically around 20–25, and were physically fit and strong, the result of endless hours of training and a diet that was better than the average, being especially high in meat. Tactically the armies were similar in being unused to fighting together in such large hosts, with the resources needed to equip and maintain a force of any appreciable size being of such magnitude that it would tax a state to its very limit. To then risk such an incredibly expensive asset in open battle was a decision fraught with danger; a major defeat would be nothing less than a national catastrophe, Hardrada's annihilation at Stamford Bridge destroyed Norway's military capability for more than a generation, while Anglo-Saxon England never recovered from Hastings of course.

Hastings was no long drawn-out campaign, there were not a large number of skirmishes and sieges. More than anything William needed a quick battle that would prove decisive, and Harold gave him exactly that. On the day, in essence, England's fate would be decided in a straight contest between the power, aggression and tactical brilliance of a sophisticated all-arms Franco-Norman army, and the resolute steadfastness of the English housecarle and his shield wall – but after having fought two major battles in the weeks before, it would not be enough, and England would fall.

THE DAYS BEFORE
THE BATTLE

King Harold was under no illusions as to the precariousness of his new throne, but of his two opponents he considered William's Normandy the greater threat, hence he called out the southern fyrd and its naval counterpart that summer and strung garrisons out all along England's south coast waiting to sight the Norman invasion fleet. William meanwhile was eager not to disappoint and after securing papal support and security for his duchy from its neighbours, he set about building an armada and assembling the men to fill it. He would take an army across the Channel of some 7000 or more men, well over 2000 horses, and all the paraphernalia of an army on campaign; food, wine, beer, tentage, tools, spare weapons and armour, camp furniture, clothes, and so on. The importance of logistics in war can never be overerestimated, and William had to prepare for a landing on a hostile shore where no-one would be rushing to resupply him. On top of all this he had to actually build his fleet almost from scratch. As a coastal region, Normandy had the usual coterie of fishing boats, but it had no naval tradition and what ships were available were wholly unsuited to the task. The call went out for shipwrights and carpenters, and in a matter of months some 700 or more ships were floating in the waters of the Dives estuary waiting to transport the army north. What held them in port were adverse winds, which, far to the north, had the opposite effect and swept Harold's other foes towards their goal – the Norwegians were coming.

The Battle of Fulford

At the beginning of August, King Harald Hardrada's army left its anchorage in the Solund Islands north of Bergen and headed over to the Shetlands and the Orkneys. Following the time-honoured Viking route it then hopped across to Scotland at Duncansby Head and began to move down the east coast, gathering allies as it went. Men and ships flocked to Hardrada from across the Norse colonies and settlements, swelling his army to perhaps 500 ships and 10,000 men. Desperate to reclaim power and position in England, Northumbria's deposed earl, Tostig, joined Hardrada with a few hundred supporters as the host made its way down England's east coast, plundering and burning its way south. Reaching the Humber it sailed up the great estuary and into the Ouse, making landfall at the village of Riccall, some eight miles south of York on 19 September.

Forewarned by the raids farther north, Morcar – Tostig's replacement as Earl of Northumbria – had concentrated his forces behind York's stout walls. He had been joined by his brother Edwin, the Earl of Mercia, and several thousand of his men, so that the two noblemen commanded around 6–7000 men in total. They sent word south to King Harold of Hardrada's invasion, but realistically could not expect any reinforcements for several weeks, particularly as Harold had just given orders to disband the southern fyrd when William's invasion failed to materialise. The two young earls, untried and both under 20 at the time, were faced with a decision. Either they sat back, defended York and waited for Harold to appear and relieve them, or they marched out to face the Thunderbolt of the North. The decision they made was ultimately fatal for Anglo-Saxon England.

Disregarding the instructions from their king to keep their army intact and await his arrival, on the morning of Wednesday

SCANDINAVIAN DIASPORA

The dawning of the Viking Age was partly due to a
population explosion in their native Scandinavia
that forced the inhabitants to leave their own
shores, with the same phenomenon occurring again
in the nineteenth century when almost 3 million
Scandinavians migrated to the United States, primarily
to Wisconsin, Minnesota and Michigan. These periodic
migrations depressed the home populations so that by
1400 there were only around 140,000 people living in
Norway, and even today, Norway's population stands at
less than five million compared to the UK's 65 million.

20 September the military might of northern England marched
away from York's protective fortifications and headed south along
what is now the A19. The two teenagers would now face a huge
Norse army commanded by the experienced 40-year-old Tostig
Godwinson and an old man of 51 who was recognised as one of
the greatest warriors of the age – Harald Hardrada Sigurdsson.

The two armies came into sight of one another near Fulford,
now a suburb of York, then a small village. Like the rest of the
Vale of York the land is low-lying, criss-crossed with streams and
brooks, with thick clay soil that when wet becomes a struggle
to cross. In this landscape high ground is militarily key terrain,
and it was the hugely experienced Norseman who spotted that
a low ridge running from left to right between the two armies
dominated the area. He immediately ordered his men to move
onto it and deploy into line. For such large forces there was very
little room for manoeuvre for either, with the Ouse on the Norse
left and a dyke and marshland on their right. Hardrada positioned
himself near the river with the cream of his own troops, including
his son Olaf and his loyal lieutenant Eystein Orri, who was not only
betrothed to Hardrada's daughter Maria, but whose sister Thora
was the king's mistress.

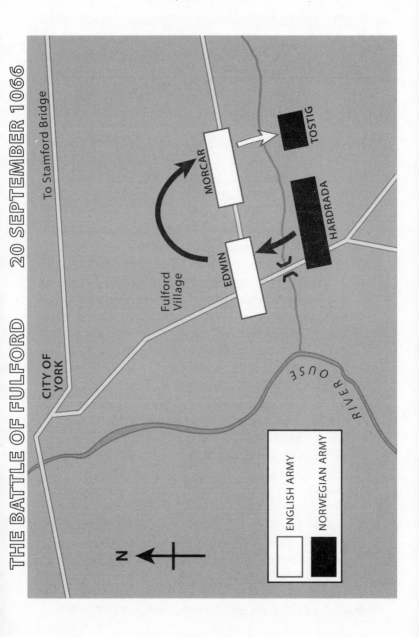

THE BATTLE OF FULFORD   20 SEPTEMBER 1066

To Stamford Bridge

TOSTIG

MORCAR

HARDRADA

EDWIN

Fulford Village

CITY OF YORK

RIVER OUSE

ENGLISH ARMY

NORWEGIAN ARMY

N

Tostig and his English carles were left to command the far-weaker right wing. The northern English drew up in their traditional shield wall and advanced, Edwin and his Mercians against Harald's left wing, and Morcar's Northumbrians facing Tostig on the right. Morcar and his men, many of whom would have had Scandinavian blood running through their veins, pressed hard into their opponents and the outnumbered English and Norse steadily gave way, while Harald's left wing held their ground against Edwin's assault. A gap appeared in the English line as Morcar's men outpaced their Mercian brethren, and this sealed the fate of the army. Harald had been waiting for just this moment, and he led his men into a savage counter-attack straight into the Northumbrian's exposed flank. The English army was sundered in two, with the Northumbrians pinned against a web of streams, swamps and ditches. Unable to escape they were butchered in their thousands. The Anglo-Saxon Chronicle barely mentions the battle unfortunately, the best account we have being the *Heimskringla* saga written by the Icelander Snorri Sturluson in the thirteenth century, it says:

> The Norwegian onslaught was so fierce that everything gave way before it, and a great number of the English were killed. The English army quickly broke into flight, some fleeing up the river, and others down the river, but most of them fled into the swamp, where the dead piled up so thickly that the Norwegians could cross the swamp dry-shod.

The majority of the finest troops in Mercia and Northumbria, including a large number of irreplaceable housecarles, were killed at Fulford. Their place in the shield wall at Hastings would be taken by less well equipped and experienced select fyrd men, who would prove unequal to the task. As such, Fulford was a hammer blow for Harold.

The day after the battle York surrendered and Anglo-Saxon England seemed at the mercy of the Norsemen. King Harold then proceeded to carry out one of the most daring and ultimately successful military feats of the era. Alerted by Edwin and Morcar's messengers, he had already moved to London from the south coast to collect more troops, and then without hesitation he set off north up Ermine Street, the old Roman military road, to cover the 200 miles to York and face the Norwegians.

The popular misconception is that Harold and his men marched all the way to York and then back again, and hence they were all exhausted when they faced William at Hastings, but this is not the case. Harold arrived at Tadcaster with its vital bridge over the River Wharfe, some seven miles from York, on Sunday 24 September, meaning that even had they left London before Fulford had actually been fought they would have had to cover the 190 miles from London to Tadcaster in five or six days, and therefore far exceed the approximately 25 miles a day which was then, and still is now, the maximum for a marching army. What is therefore indisputable is that Harold and his men did not traverse the country north, then south, on foot, but on horseback. Anglo-Saxon England's military might fight on their feet, but they arrived at the battlefield itself by horse. Harold did not tarry at Tadcaster but left before first light, leading his army straight through York early on the Monday morning and barring the gates behind him so news of his arrival could not be leaked to Hardrada by any of its Scandinavian residents.

The Battle of Stamford Bridge

The English headed east along what is now the A166 for about eight miles to arrive at the ridge of Gate Helmsley, and below it the River Derwent and its crossing point at the tiny hamlet of Stamford Bridge. Harold's royal army was relatively small, probably only around 5000 men, but it was his élite. With the king were his own Wessex housecarles, and those of his brother Gyrth, the Earl of East Anglia, plus a select number of southern thegns. They were joined by some hardy survivors of the disaster at Fulford,

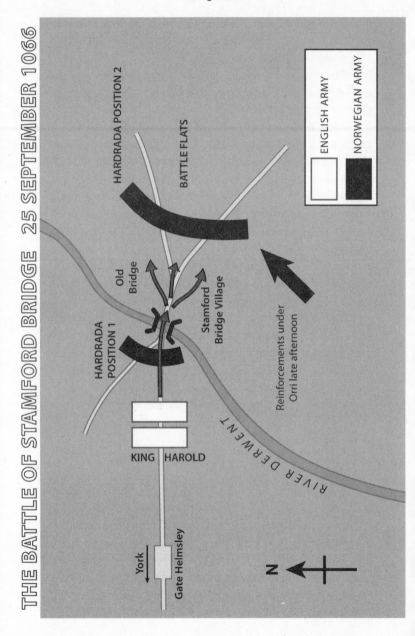

THE BATTLE OF STAMFORD BRIDGE 25 SEPTEMBER 1066

ENGLISH ARMY

NORWEGIAN ARMY

HARDRADA POSITION 2

BATTLE FLATS

Old Bridge

Stamford Bridge Village

Reinforcements under Orri late afternoon

HARDRADA POSITION 1

KING HAROLD

RIVER DERWENT

York

Gate Helmsley

N

but not by either Edwin or Morcar who didn't fight at Stamford Bridge or Hastings. The Norwegian army they faced in the valley below still outnumbered them, but Hardrada was caught totally by surprise by Harold's dash north and his men were divided and unprepared. The Norse king had sent his prospective son-in-law, Eystein Orri, south to Riccall with around 2000 men to protect the precious Viking fleet, and many others were out on foraging and plundering expeditions, no-one believing that the English could react so quickly after the butchery of Fulford. Worse still, the men he did have in the valley were camped on both the east and west banks of the river, and due to the hot weather most of them had left their precious mail *bjarnas* aboard their vessels.

Harold took full advantage of the situation, and signalled an immediate attack. Staying mounted, the English swept down the long, gentle slope towards the Derwent, sending the Norse into near panic. Harald and Tostig desperately tried to concentrate their forces on the eastern bank, while those on the western side struggled to get over the small bridge, shielded by a few brave souls who stood as rearguard. Stamford Bridge today is not too dissimilar from how it was then. The Derwent is deep and fast-flowing, about 30 feet wide, with steep and muddy banks. On the far eastern bank the land climbs gently through hedged fields to a sort of plateau now called Battle Flats. This is where the Norwegians were attempting to concentrate. The original bridge across the river was Roman and the stone pillars were still in place, covered in the eleventh century by wooden planking that was only wide enough for two men to pass at a time. Today the road bridge is still narrow, only a single lane, and is near enough in the same place. For both armies it was vital. If the English could take it they would cut the Norwegian army in two and could flood across the river, smashing into Hardrada's men before they were ready. For the Norse, if they could hold the bridge their main force would have the time to come together, form into battle line and await the reinforcements from Riccall who were instantly summoned to their king's aid. The bridge was the key to victory, and King

21. Next to the bridge at Stamford is The Swordsman Inn, which commemorates the tale of the lone giant Norseman who held the English at the bridge before being speared from below.

Harold's men charged at it. The English attacked on horseback and the fighting was ferocious. The Norwegian rearguard was cut down one by one until legend has it that a lone giant Viking was all that was left in the way of Harold's army. This courageous soul stood his ground and held the English at bay, frustrating their attempts to cross as he killed every man who came against him. Eventually an Englishman used a small boat to float underneath the bridge and thrust a spear into the giant Norseman from below and end his resistance. The English streamed across and prepared to go into battle. Harold tried to parley and offered his brother forgiveness and an earldom, whereupon Tostig asked what land his ally Hardrada would receive for his pains. King Harold's reply has become famous: 'Seven feet of English earth, or as much more, as he is taller than most men.'

Tostig refused and the battle began again with an English charge. Sturluson records that this phase of the fighting was

22. The current single lane bridge over the Derwent at Stamford Bridge shown here from the eastern bank. It is thought it stands at most some 300–400m from the original bridge site.

dominated by English cavalry, and most historians have discounted it for that reason, but it is likely that at least some of Harold's men would have stayed on horseback throwing spears and other missiles to try and weaken the Norwegian shield wall, even though the majority of his men would have been on foot. Without their precious mail shirts the Norse were hard-pressed, gaps appearing in the line as unprotected men fell victim to arrows and spears. In a desperate gamble Hardrada personally led a counter-attack under his 'Land Waster' banner of the black raven on a white background, to try and wrest the initiative back from the English. The Norse attack failed and Hardrada himself was killed, possibly by an arrow to the throat. Tostig now took command, but with their inspirational king dead, the exhausted Norse were doomed.

Surrounded, their shield wall shrinking as they stood among their own dead, they still refused to surrender. Sturluson again:

> Both sides drew back to form up again, and there was a long lull in the fighting. Before the fighting was resumed, Harold Godwinson offered quarter to his brother Tostig and all the surviving Norwegians. But the Norwegians shouted back with one voice that every one of them would rather die than accept quarter from the English; they roared their battle-cry, and the battle started again.

At this stage of the battle Eystein Orri arrived with the men from Riccall to give the Vikings renewed hope. Exhausted by their run from the fleet they were unable to stand up to the ferocity of the English housecarles, and the Norwegian line fell apart. Tostig and all his carles were killed where they stood and the Norwegians were routed with Orri himself hacked down. In desperation the survivors tried to flee back south to their ships and were cut to pieces, with perhaps as many as 7000 corpses littering the battlefield and the surrounding countryside. The slaughter was so great that only 24 of the 500 or so ships in the Viking fleet were needed to take the survivors home, and so many of Norway's aristocracy and warrior class were killed that the nation was unable to field another army of comparable size for more than a generation.

Harold was triumphant. In one remarkable day he had done something the like of which had not been achieved by an English monarch since the days of Athelstan at Brunanburh more than a century earlier. So complete was his victory that it effectively signalled the end of the Viking Age in England, and had history stopped at Stamford Bridge then Harold would rightly have been lauded as one of England's greatest ever warrior-kings.

Instead, some 250 miles to the south, an army was wading ashore on Pevensey's long shingle beach. That army had spent what was probably several months cooped up on the shores of Normandy waiting for the winds and weather that would drive

23. *Battle Flats plateau looking away to the east as Harold's army would have seen it as they swarmed up from the river. The Norse shield wall was bent round at this point to try and stop the English from outflanking them.*

24. *Battle Flats looking down towards the river Derwent. The slope is not steep and would not have impeded the English as they charged the unarmoured Norsemen and their English allies under Tostig. Also present was Copsi, a trusted lieutenant of Tostig who would survive the battle and be made Earl of Northumbria by William the Conqueror before being murdered by the local nobility just five weeks later.*

REFUGE AND BURIAL

In the aftermath of the battle the Norse survivors re-grouped in the Orkneys under Hardrada's 16-year-old son Olaf and the young Orcadian jarls Paul and Erlend Thorfinnsson, whom Harold spared provided they undertook never to invade England again. Olaf sailed home in 1067 and shared the Norwegian crown with his brother Magnus II, until Magnus's death in 1069 whereupon he became Olaf III the Peaceful, sole ruler of Norway. Hardrada's body was left in England for a whole year before being carried home and interred in St Mary's Church in Trondheim. Tostig's body was taken to York by his brother and buried at the Minster. His two sons, Skuli (14) and Ketil (12) Tostigson took refuge with their mother Judith, daughter of Count Baldwin IV of Flanders, in Norway.

them north to England. William's feat in even reaching that shore was a monumental achievement. Back in January on hearing of Edward's death and Harold's coronation, the duke had flown into a rage, railing against what he clearly saw as Harold's usurpation of his crown. His reaction was immediate and absolute – he would invade England and take the country by force. William's genius was then to recognise what he needed to achieve that goal and go and get it. An army, allies and a fleet were all assembled and put in place, but the riskiness of such a venture cannot be underestimated. William was gambling everything on this throw of the dice. He had to transport his new army to a hostile shore, and find and destroy Harold quickly before the campaigning season ended and winter set in, with little hope of any reinforcement or re-supply from his duchy.

At first it seemed as if fortune had deserted the duke. The winds were against him, and when they finally turned on 12 September the fleet had barely reached open water before another change in the weather scattered it during the night, wrecking a number

25. *The Norman invasion fleet crosses the English Channel.*

HORSE SENSE

While transporting the cavalry mounts was crucial, the actual mechanics of loading thousands of powerful, skittish horses onto ships was a huge challenge. To achieve it the Normans turned to military engineering and dug earthen ramps from the sea-shore out to form jetties. One by one their ships came alongside and the precious horses were simply led along the ramps and could then step down into the holds and be made secure. The Normans used the same technique at Oranto in Italy in 1061 as they prepared to attack Byzantine Sicily.

26. *Dives-sur-Mer, where the Norman fleet assembled in preparation for the invasion of England.*

of vessels and sending the rest scrabbling into the safe harbour of St Valéry-sur-Somme. The army was close to losing heart, but as usual William's leadership was steely. William of Poitiers recounts how the duke dealt with the episode: 'Warding off adversity by prudence, he kept secret as far as possible the deaths of those whom the waves had engulfed and had them buried in secret.'

The canny Norman lord also doubled the men's wine and meat rations and even paraded the embalmed body of St Valéry himself round his army's tents to try and lift the men's spirits, and just when all seemed lost, the wind changed. Dawn on 27 September broke clear and dry, and after waiting for 45 days in the rain, mud and wind the Franco-Norman army embarked aboard their new fleet with undisguised relief, and sailed north. With each ship bearing a lantern on their masthead the armada sailed through the night, losing only two ships in the darkness.Come the dawn, the last successful invasion fleet to reach England' shores were beaching on Pevensey's long and softly shelving beach.

27. French cavalry horses are disembarked on the English coast.

28. Bishop Odo blesses a meal at the French camp.

MYTHS AND PORTENTS

The invasion is embroidered with a host of tales, some of which we know to be true, others are almost certainly pure invention. Three of the most famous are during his time in Normandy Harold swore on holy relics to support William as the future king, the appearance of a blazing star in the sky as an omen in 1066, and William falling to his knees on Pevensey beach and declaring he held England in his hands as he grasped the sand. The blazing star is true, it was Halley's comet, the last is pure myth, however the first may be true, although it may well have been invented to support William's rightful claim in the eyes of God and the papacy.

Stretching away from the landing beach were miles of tidal flats, nowadays protected by a shingle breakwater, and here William disembarked his army and began as the Normans meant to go on – they built a fort. Robert Wace, a Jersey-born Norman writing around 1160 described the scene:

> Then the carpenters landed. They had great axes in their hands, and planes and adzes hung at their sides. They had brought with them from Normandy the elements of three wooden forts, ready for putting together. It was all shaped and pierced to take the pins they had brought cut and ready in large barrels. Before evening had set in they had completed a good fort on English soil and there they placed their stores. Everyone then ate and drank well, right glad that they were ashore.

This first Norman toehold in England was erected within the existing walls and ditch of the old Roman fortress of Anderida. It would be the first of hundreds of fortifications that would come to characterise Norman England over the coming centuries. With King Harold recovering in York after his victory at Stamford Bridge

29. Pevensey Beach. Here at what is now called Normans Bay, William and his army came ashore. The bay is long and sheltered and perfect for landing troops and supplies.

30. Stretching away for several miles inland from Pevensey Beach are the tidal flats, drained now, but in 1066 they were not ideal territory for heavily armed soldiers and their horses.

31. The old Roman fort of Anderida (modern-day Pevensey). Garrisoned by the Romano-Britons after Rome's departure, it was destroyed by a Saxon raid. William occupied it and built the first Norman keep inside the Roman walls and ditch.

and the local fyrd disbanded after the summer long stand-to, the Normans were left unmolested and able to move unhindered east along the coast to the more suitable base of Hastings. From here William needed to move north, find Harold and win the kingdom.

At the time there was just a single ancient track that ran north to the primeval Andredsweald forest and the Roman road to London and England's heartlands. That track followed the high ground north-west to little more than a hump in the rolling countryside, a low hill called Caldbec. Copses, knolls, streams and marshland criss-crossed the land, making it close country, green and fertile. It was here, among the rabbit warrens and coarse scrub, that England's fate would be decided.

32. Pevensey Castle. The medieval keep was built on the old motte and bailey wooden construction first placed there by William's carpenters.

Two hundred miles to the north, King Harold and his surviving carles and fyrd men were still binding their wounds after shattering the Norse. Having lost maybe as many as 3000 of his very best men killed or wounded at the Derwent just six days earlier, the king was handed a message on 1 October telling him his worst fears had come true – William had landed. There are no surviving records of Harold's reaction, although we can only surmise his feelings as he looked around at the bloodied remnants of his army, knowing perhaps their greatest trial was yet to come. He did not hesitate. As his own men prepared for further battle, messengers were sent out that very night summoning those select fyrds who had not marched north, telling them to meet the king in the south. Gathering his weary veterans, Harold Godwinson climbed into the saddle the following morning and headed back south to repel a second invader. He had been king for less than eight months.

33. Moving away from Pevensey, William marched his army along the coast to the far better site of Hastings. Here he ordered the erection of another fort.

THE BATTLE

The Battle of Hastings, without any doubt the most important battle ever fought on English soil and arguably the most historically significant in English history, was not actually fought there. A modern visitor to Hastings will on enquiry be directed seven miles to the northwest along the A21 and A2100 to the picturesque town of Battle, founded in the aftermath of 1066 in commemoration. It was here on a clear, warm day in mid-October that Duke William and King Harold would meet and decide England's future in a welter of bloodshed.

The battle's name is just one of a barrel of mysteries surrounding that fateful day. The biggest by far was why the battle was even fought at all. William was desperate for it. He had taken his army across the Channel and was now effectively stranded. He had thousands of men and horses who would go through food, water and forage at a prodigious rate, and could not be re-supplied or reinforced from back home in Normandy. Almost immediately on landing, his men were burning, looting and pillaging the local area, as the Bayeux Tapestry illustrates, stripping them of the supplies his men needed and condemning the Sussex villagers to destitution and starvation in the coming winter.

Time was William's greatest enemy. It was late in the season and he needed a single, decisive battle and victory to give him a chance

34. This scene from the Bayeux Tapestry did not shy away from showing the Normans burning the houses of locals in the Sussex countryside. It was a pattern they would continue throughout England and would reach its zenith – or rather, nadir – in the Harrying of the North.

at the crown. For Harold the opposite was true. Time was on the Anglo-Saxon's side. There was no Humber estuary on the south coast, no route way into the English heartlands, Harold could have screened William, pinning him against the sea and simply waited him out, starving his army into submission and a humiliating withdrawal. Instead he went straight at William. Covering around 40 miles a day he arrived in London with his carles on the evening of 6 October. His messengers had done their job, and men from the select fyrds across the southeast, the lower midlands and even the southwest were starting to appear to swell the king's army.

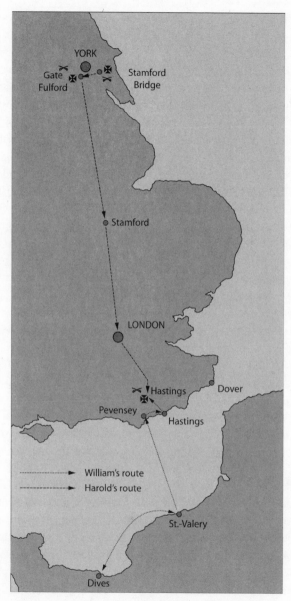

35. *The routes taken by William and Harold to Hastings.*

The headstrong monarch tarried for less than a week before he decided enough was enough and it was time to face his rival. His younger brother Gyrth, the Earl of East Anglia, tried to persuade the king to stay in London and let him take the army south so that no matter what, the king would be safe, but Harold dismissed the idea out of hand. Harold's decision to charge out of London and head south has never been explained, with conflicting views abounding, his desire to save the local populace from further Norman depredations being amongst the most unlikely. Whatever the cause, the fact was that Harold led an army out of London, probably on the morning of 12 October, that was at most 7000 men strong, with only perhaps a little over 3000 of those men being hauberk-equipped frontline housecarles, lithsmen or thegns who had fought at Stamford Bridge. These men were still recovering from the cataclysm on the Derwent and the loss there of as many as half of their friends and comrades, while the rest of the army were select fyrd men predominantly from the southern shires; well-equipped and with some experience, but untried and facing the sternest of tests. With the king rode his brothers Gyrth and Leofwine with their retinues, but of Edwin and Morcar there was no sign, and the two great earldoms of Mercia and Northumbria would be almost wholly absent from Hastings. According to the Anglo-Saxon Chronicle, King Harold had given orders that the army was to move approximately 60 miles and assemble on 13 October 'at the hoar apple-tree', a well-known local landmark at the boundary of the Sussex hundreds of Baldslow, Ninfield and Hailesaltede on the far side of a massive primeval forest, the Andredsweald, which stretched for some 80 miles from Petersfield in Hampshire in the east, all the way to Ashford in Kent in the west. It was rarely less than 15 miles deep along its length. The apple tree has long gone of course, but there is little doubt that the location is modern-day Caldbec Hill, at 300 feet above sea-level the dominating feature in the area. All was bustle as in the gathering gloom of the evening of the 13th as the army began to arrive and prepare for the confrontation they knew would come

36. Hastings today.

the following day. All that night more men arrived, tethered their horses, ate their evening meal and tried to snatch a few hours sleep, but it was almost daybreak before the end of the column reached the assembly point, and for those poor souls there would be no time to rest. Rising with the dawn, King Harold mustered his men and set off south, hoping to catch William unawares as he had with the Norse at Stamford Bridge just over a fortnight earlier.

It was not to be. Ever the prudent commander, William had scouts out in numbers, they discovered the presence of the English army and the duke was informed without delay. For William the arrival of Harold and his main army was a godsend. There would be no need to cautiously advance north and try and force the king to battle while the Franco-Norman army was still in its prime, their enemy was but a few miles away and a decisive action

37. The gatehouse of Battle Abbey. In 1070 Pope Alexander II ordered William to do penance for killing so many people during the conquest of England. William began to build the abbey, dedicating it to St Martin, sometimes known as 'the Apostle of the Gauls', but he died before it was completed. Its church was finished in about 1094 and consecrated during the reign of his son William Rufus.

could be fought now when it suited William the most. Mirroring Harold exactly, William had his men up and moving out of their encampment before sunrise on the morning of 14 October. As the sun rose around 6.30am on a warm, still day, the Norman and English armies were heading towards each other at pace, both sides eager for the clash and believing the day would be theirs. The result of such eagerness was a battle that was almost a meeting engagement, with neither side having the time to carry out extensive reconnaissance or, for the English, to prepare their position with any fortifications such as a ditch or sharpened stakes. When his own scouts reported the Normans were on the march, Harold, with the benefit of local knowledge, led his men forward on foot and opted to position his army on a ridgeline running east-west just about a mile forward of Caldbec Hill.

38. The original cloisters of Battle Abbey.

Battle Hill is no mountain, but it is an imposing position and one well suited to an infantry defence of the shield wall. At its top is a fairly flat plateau, some 800 metres long and about 150 metres deep. It is protected on its flanks and rear by a number of streams and areas of marshy ground that fall away, sometimes pretty steeply, giving an attacker little choice but to go for a frontal assault up the slope that stretches away below the ridgeline for 400–500 metres. This is no easy option, with more streams and boggy ground to negotiate at the base of that same slope, before an army then has to struggle up the incline to the summit itself. Over the centuries the monks of Battle Abbey terraced the hill to a degree, especially at the summit to build the Abbey itself, but the feature remains essentially the same, with the gradient steepest in the centre and eastern side, at around 1 in 15, and far less so at its western end where it reduces to 1 in 33. In practical

BATTLE OR CALDBEC?

Following the battle, the Pope ordered William to do penance for the loss of life by building an abbey on the site itself. The high altar was positioned on the spot where Harold was meant to have fallen, and hence the traditional site of the battle has been fixed as Battle Abbey. There is some controversy among historians about this, with many pointing out that it would have made sense for Harold to use Caldbec Hill itself as it is higher and would have been the more natural site for the shield wall. Indeed, the Anglo-Saxon Chronicle states; 'he (Harold) assembled a large army and came against at the hoary apple tree', which we know to be Caldbec Hill. While Orderic Vitalis wrote: 'Suddenly the forest poured forth troops of men, and from the hiding places of the woods a host dashed forward. There was a hill near the forest … they sized this place for the battle. On the highest point of the summit Harold planted his banner.' This could be Caldbec, but Battle is the most likely site.

terms anyone can walk up it without undue effort, even carrying the equivalent of the additional weight of arms and armour. For cavalry, however, the slope would prove a hindrance, although conversely it would allow them to disengage quickly if they were to turn away and retreat downhill. This would prove incredibly useful during the battle. Archers too would suffer, as they would be forced to shoot upwards and hence lose much of the impact of their volleys. On the other hand, if Harold had had a large number of his own bowmen they would have been doubly effective, a lack of capability the English would come to rue.

However, by far the biggest feature of the battleground that strikes anyone who has walked it is its compactness. Other famous battles such as El Alamein, Kursk, the Somme and so on, were fought over areas measured in tens of square of miles, if not hundreds. Hastings, on the other hand, can be measured in the hundreds of metres. The battle was to last all day, and at no

39, 40, 41. The battlefield today from the summit of Battle Hill, approximately where Harold had drawn up the English army. As can be seen the slope is not hugely steep but would without doubt impede cavalry and give the defender an advantage.

42. An English scout warns King Harold of the Normans' approach.

time were the men who fought it more than a couple of football pitches away from each other.

While King Harold was hurriedly forming his line on the ridge, William was just over a mile away near Telham Hill and its neighbour Blackhorse Hill, hidden from view by woods on either side of the same track the English had used to come south. Just as Harold's scouts had warned him of the Norman advance, so William's scouts told him of the English situation. Still out of sight, the duke halted his army and instructed them to prepare for battle while he rode forward to get a view of his enemy. So as his men donned their precious, but heavy, hauberks, William and his retinue galloped round the bend in the road and as the valley opened up in front of him he caught his first sight of the English army. It must have been an imposing sight with Harold's 7000 or so men crammed onto the ridgeline above him in ranks

43. The feared shield wall of English housecarles at Hastings. The single unarmoured archer is the only depiction on the entire Bayeux Tapestry of English bowmen, with his size signifying low social status as well as lack of numbers.

up to ten or twelve deep. The morning sun glinted off thousands of spear points, helmets and mailshirts, and above it all right in the centre fluttered two enormous banners; the Wyvern (dragon of Wessex) and the famed 'Fighting Man' – Harold's personal totem.

William had not come to England to be overawed at the site of a shield wall, but cast his general's eye over the terrain and his opponent. It was obvious that Harold had decided to stay on the defensive and use the ridge to his advantage, so that cast William in the role of the attacker, a position he relished, and within minutes he had decided on his plan and rode back to his men to give them his orders for the assault.

THE BANNERS

The 'Dragon of Wessex' was a two-legged upright winged dragon, or Wyvern, probably red. While the 'Fighting Man' was the heroic figure of an English warrior with shield and sword, all picked out in precious stones and gold thread. After the battle the Fighting Man was presented to William, who almost certainly sent it on to the Pope in Rome. As for the Wessex dragon it disappeared.

Those orders were crucial, and showed William to be both a hugely talented leader as well as a man willing to take a calculated risk. The foot of the slope in front of the English, Senlac or Santlache as it was known, was girded by two streams and surrounding marshes, totally unsuitable for cavalry and infantrymen wearing heavy armour.

The track the Normans were on ran through Santlache on a narrow 200m-wide ribbon of dry ground, which had to be crossed in column to bring William's army to the foot of Battle Hill. The men would then have to form up in line on the other side in full view of the English, no more than a few hundred metres away on the summit. If Harold attacked during this manoeuvre then he could possibly cut the Normans in two and destroy them piecemeal. William knew the risk, and took it. He had already divided his army into three distinct sections, breaking it down into manageable units to give him strong and clear command and control, and these units would be his manoeuvre sections for the forthcoming action. The vanguard was commanded by William's Norman Companion, Roger de Montgomerie, and was made up of 1500 or so mercenaries and allied troops from Flanders and northern France, as well as a small number of Normans under Robert de Beaumont (son of William's ally Roger de Beaumont).

They moved off first, passing through the gap and then swinging east to take up position on the right of the Norman line as they

44, 45, 46. The battlefield today from the Normans' point of view at the bottom of Battle Hill looking up to Harold's shield wall. The ground is mostly open but on the left becomes quite broken and uneven; this is where Count Alan and his Bretons stood.

THE FOOT OF THE SLOPE?

It is this patch of ground that gave rise to the name 'Senlac' that is sometimes used to describe the battle site itself. Originally known at the time as 'Santlache', or 'Sanlacu', it literally means 'sand-lake', and was later bastardised to 'Senlac'. Much of the marshland in the area has been drained over the centuries so the exact location of 'Senlac' and identification of what it really was is still imprecise.

looked up the hill. Next went the duke's ally, Count Alan of Brittany, with 2000 Bretons, Poitevins, Angevins and men from the County of Maine, who swung west and formed the Franco-Norman left wing facing the English up the shallowest gradient. Last to take up position was William himself, leading the strongest division, the 3500-strong Norman core of the army, with a preponderance of armoured cavalry and heavy infantry. They looked up directly at The Fighting Man, King Harold and his personal housecarles, and together they linked William's line together into one cohesive whole. With this bold manoeuvre William had stolen the initiative, and he would not relinquish it for the rest of the battle.

As for Harold, he remained entirely passive, deciding not to intervene when the Normans were clearly vulnerable. True, it would have meant giving up the advantage of the high ground, but he had taken exactly that same risk at Stamford Bridge and it had brought him a magnificent victory; this time he simply stood by. As for his battle strategy, the English plan was simplicity itself and was entirely based on the traditional Germanic tactic of the shield wall, also called the 'war-hedge'. The men were formed into a single, huge rectangular block, in rough rows, with each man taking up about three feet so that he had enough room to use his spear and shield, although the men armed with swords and axes had to be ever mindful of the men around them less they injure their own. The front rank was the most important of course, as it would take

CAVALRY NUMBERS

Whilst we have estimated heavy cavalry numbers here, it is extremely difficult to be sure. They appear in the Bayeux Tapestry more than the other types of combatants, but then they are more visually dramatic and therefore were probably an attractive subject for the Tapestry's makers. As the historian M.K. Lawson points out, 'analogies prove nothing, but it is worth noting that probably under 10 per cent of the men whom Caesar led against Britain in 54 BC were horsemen.' However, the Roman army was an infantry one, whereas William's was not.

47. French cavalry prepare to go into battle.

the brunt of the enemy's charge, so these men were all professional warriors, housecarles and lithsmen, and were equipped to a man with hauberks. The same was true of the second rank and some of the third rank. These men were vital. Their armour was proof against most missiles such as arrows and throwing spears, and their mail-shirted bulk would shield the mass of the army behind them. If these men fell, the future of Anglo-Saxon England would lie with the select fyrd contingents of southern England standing behind them, whose padded leather jackets and quilted jerkins would be no match for Norman cavalry spears and infantry swords, which would wreak havoc in their ranks. As long as the famed housecarles stood then the shield wall was nigh on impregnable and the day would belong to the English.

Although the men were arrayed in rows, they were also grouped by shires and feudal dues; the men from Kent stood together, as did those contingents from London, Sussex, Bedfordshire, Surrey, Essex, Buckinghamshire and Berkshire. As for Harold's brothers, the Earls Gyrth and Leofwine, the majority of their best men were front rankers, but they themselves stood slightly back from the front with a small number of their own carles, as did all the other Saxon nobles and thegns. Their personal banners fluttered above them, but all were overshadowed by the King's Wessex dragon and Fighting Man as he stood right in the centre of his army on the highest point of Battle Hill, surrounded by the pick of his warriors, everyone one of them a veteran of Harold's Welsh wars and Stamford Bridge.

The contrast between the dispositions of the two armies could not have been greater. William was using a sophisticated structure for his forces, specifically tailored to provide him with command and control and enabling him to adapt to any changes in the forthcoming battle. In comparison, Harold had effectively surrendered control of his army to the vagaries of the day. His ability to manoeuvre, launch counter-attacks or even reinforce sections of his own line was non-existent. It is a puzzle that will never be answered as to why a commander of Harold's experience

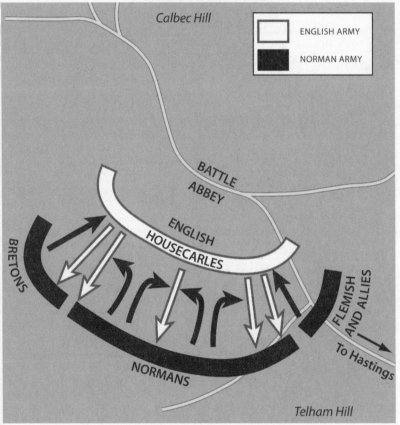

THE BATTLE OF HASTINGS
14 OCTOBER 1066

48. The Battle of Hastings, 14 October 1066.

and track record adopted a battle plan based entirely on the hope his men would stand and outlast the Norman assault.

The two armies now faced each other less than 300 metres apart. Housecarles, lithsmen, Normans, Bretons and Flemings would have been able to make out individuals in the ranks facing them, and no doubt insults and jibes were traded as the men built

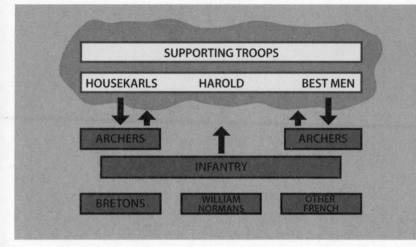

up their courage for the ordeal to come. The Franco-Norman army was in a rough line now, grouped into compact and manageable units gathered around their own lords, ensuring they would fight alongside men they knew and had trained with. They began to edge forward up the hill, their commanders keeping them in check, while above them the same was true of the English, the shield wall ebbing and flowing like a living thing, men shouting and standing on each other's feet, swords and scabbards banging against shields and legs, all of them just waiting.

Just as King Harold knew his task that day was to hold the line, Duke William also knew exactly what he had to do to win – kill the English housecarles. Do that and England was his, and he would no longer be a mere duke; he would be a king. And so, at 9 o'clock in the morning, with the blare of trumpets, William ordered the battle to begin.

Unsurprisingly, given the make-up of his forces, William's first attack was led by his heavy infantry supported by hundreds of archers loosing volley after volley at the English line. Orderic described how 'the Norman infantry closed to attack the English', and Guy of Amiens has the Norman archers firing 'at the faces of the English', with those armed with crossbows 'destroying the shields of the English as if by a hailstorm'. Expensive hauberks and kite shields did their job – but still some men fell, quarrels and arrows punching home into eyes and necks.

With few archers of their own, the English had no choice but to wait until the Normans were within 20–30 metres at most before they could reply, and then they began to hurl their throwing spears. The slope gave them an advantage, and Normans were bowled off their feet, tumbling back down the hill. Their comrades stepped over their bodies and carried on, shouting their war-cry, 'God aid us!' The English responded with their own ancient Saxon call of 'Out! Out! Out!' Then, when the Normans were a few yards away the English loosed more missiles; hand-axes and large rocks prised from the hillside, and with a roar and the thud of metal and wood coming together the two armies clashed. Poitiers said, 'The noise of the shouting from the Normans on one side and the barbarians on the other could barely be heard above the clash of weapons and the groans of the dying.'

There was nothing subtle about shield wall fights, no room for decorous sword play or fancy footwork; it was a question of brute force and raw courage. The front ranks of both armies ground their shields against each other, the men behind leaning into the backs of the men in front to add their weight to the fray. Spears and knives were the preferred weapons, the Saxon *scramasax* being especially useful, as the warriors searched out weak points and gaps in armour around necks, faces, legs and hands, worrying and sawing the blades back and forth until blood flowed. So tightly packed were the combatants that sometimes the bodies of the dead and wounded were unable to fall and stayed crushed between their fellows.

The Norman infantry were taking heavy losses and the English line was holding steady, as Guy recounted: 'They bravely stood and repulsed those who were engaging them at close quarters,' so William decided to throw his cavalry into the fight to try and decide the battle quickly. With the slope against them the heavy horses could not achieve a gallop and by the time they reached

49. *The Norman cavalry charge the English shield wall. A housecarle can clearly be seen wielding the dreaded two-handed battleaxe, and the Normans cavalrymen are holding their spears overhand rather than underhand and couching them. These men were preparing to throw their lances, not drive them home.*

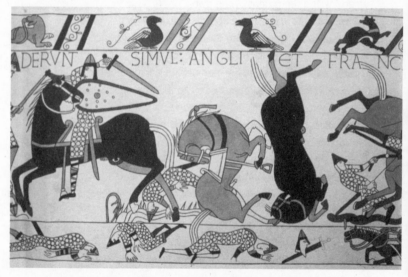

50. *The Norman cavalry are repulsed, men and horses tumbling over each other as they flee in the face of the ferocity of the English defence.*

the struggling lines of warriors they were probably doing no more than a fast canter. The technique of the mounted knight charging home with a lengthy lance couched underarm was still in its infancy, and whilst some attacked in that fashion the Bayeux Tapestry makes it clear that the vast majority of Norman cavalrymen held their lances overhand above their heads and either threw them or stabbed downwards using their height to add power. Englishmen fell, but the élite cavalry were assailed by a weapon of such ferocity that they were thrown into confusion – the two-handed battleaxe. These fearsome blades, wielded by powerful housecarles with years of training behind them, cut through hauberks, shields, horses and men. As horses fell, kicking and whinnying in agony, the Franco-Norman assault began to falter. Poitiers again: 'They [the English] began to drive them back' and 'almost the whole of Duke William's battle line fell back.'

Men fell back from the fury of the Saxon defence, and on the left Count Alan's Bretons, Poitevins and Angevins turned and ran. This left William's central division exposed on its flank, and the English came forward, ripping into the Normans. The Franco-Norman army was in danger of disintegrating, and in the chaos the cry went up that Duke William himself had been killed and near panic set in. Standing in his saddle, the Duke pulled off his helmet so his men could see him, and according to William of Poitiers he shouted:

Look at me. I am living and with God's help I shall be victor! What madness leads you to flight? What retreat do you have if you flee? If you keep going not a single one of you will escape.

While some men streamed by him, the Duke's bravery caused many of his own men to stop fleeing and rally on their leader. The Hastings battle legend taught to every school child is that this retreat was actually a deliberate Norman trick to lure the inexperienced English militiamen out from behind their protective shield wall and into a trap. The chroniclers and the Bayeux Tapestry are clear on this – this first Norman flight was real. It was true

51. The Franco-Norman army panics, and Duke William can be seen here second from the left raising his helmet to show his men he is still alive and to give them heart.

that the tactic of the feigned flight was something of a Norman speciality, and one they employed back in France – and it would be used at Hastings – but not at this point in the day. This flight was no ruse, but was caused by English skill at arms and the casualties wrought by that skill. The Bretons in particular lost a great deal of men (the Tapestry has cavalrymen tumbling over their horses' heads) in the marshland and among the uneven ground on the western side of the slope.

The bigger question is whether this English sally was a wild pursuit born of inexperience, or a deliberate counter-attack ordered by the King or one of his chief lieutenants. If it was the latter then it was the only time during the entire battle that the English deviated from their 'stand and fight' strategy. Whether deliberate or not, it ended in disaster for the English. William had steadied his men and now he turned them loose on the pursuing Saxons. Finding their courage again, the Normans drove into the flank of the pursuing English on the left. In open ground, without the protection of the shield wall, the charging Englishmen were doomed.

52. An artist's impression of the battle. It shows the possible steepness of Battle Hill before it was levelled out with terracing and the building of the Abbey.

They tried to form a shield wall on a small hillock below the main battle-line, but as the Tapestry makes clear these warriors wore no hauberks, almost certainly meaning that they were select fyrd and not trained carles. The Norman cavalrymen used their height advantage to slash down onto Saxon heads, and with no support from the rest of the army, the shield-ring was cut to pieces within minutes, and the fyrdmen were butchered to the last man. The effect on English morale can only be imagined. Barely moments ago it had seemed as if they were on the brink of victory with the Normans in headlong retreat, and now they had been forced to stand and watch as a large number of their own had been slaughtered just a few hundred yards away. The battle was now at stalemate.

53. Unarmoured and relatively inexperienced select fyrdmen thought they had the Normans beaten and ran down the hill after them. The Norman cavalry rallied, turned and cut them off. The desperate English tried to form a new, mini shield wall, but to no avail, and they were butchered to a man.

Having been fighting for the best part of two hours (most battles of the age would have been over by now) the men on both sides were exhausted and bloody. The first Norman assault had been repulsed, but so had the English counter-attack, if that was indeed what it was. Both sides had already suffered hundreds of casualties, the Tapestry depicting headless corpses and hacked off limbs, and so it is likely that the armies took pause to catch their breath – then, yet again, it was William and not Harold who seized the initiative.

Realising that any delay worked in Harold's favour rather than his, the Duke adopted a strategy of straightforward attrition. Remembering the key to the battle lay with the housecarles in the first few English ranks, he ordered all three divisions to launch repeated attacks, cavalry followed by infantry, followed by cavalry, followed by infantry and so on, and all the time the Norman archers were ordered to pepper the English war-hedge with arrows.

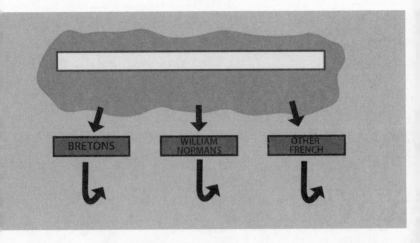

These tactics allowed the Normans to continually feed fresh troops into the line and rest between assaults, while their opponents among the English élite had no such luxury. This was no grand, cinematic charge up the hill by 2000 Norman cavalry but rather, relatively small groups of knights attacking different sections of the English shield wall in continuous relays for the next few hours. The Normans would gallop forward as fast as the slope would let them, throw their javelins, and then wheel away to be succeeded by a volley of arrows and then a second wave of heavy infantry, fighting the housecarles chest to chest. The same process was then repeated again and again, hour after hour, all along the line.

The front rank of carles had stayed solid during the first Franco-Norman assault. Their kite shields reached almost to the ground, the men hunching down behind them so only their eyes and the tops of their helmeted heads presented any sort of target. Their right hands were drawn back holding heavy war-spears, ready to thrust them forward. They were still confident. These were the men who had beaten Grufydd's Welsh warriors in the wilds of Powys, and had turned Battle Flats red with Norse blood, and they would be hard to beat now. Norman arrows fell out of the

54. *Unlike the English the Normans had a large number of archers; one of them is shown wearing mail armour and hence is of relatively high social status.*

sky, forcing them to raise their shields, as the Norman infantry closed in again. Bringing their shields back down a few arrows found their mark, slicing into shoulders and legs, as men fell a second ranker would step forward to take his place and the wall was whole again. As the two lines of infantry clashed, men stabbing at each other, snarling like animals, cohorts of cavalry would come forward at pace, the horsemen riding to within yards of the battling ranks and, picking their moment they would let fly a javelin to bury itself in the neck of a carle thrusting forward with his own spear. Gurgling his own lifeblood away the carle would fall backwards, and again another man would step forward to take his place in the line, keeping the Normans at bay. Every

55. Bishop Odo urges on the Norman soldiers, while in the background a Saxon is speared by a horseman.

once in a while a Norman cavalryman, grown overconfident, would venture too close to the English line and suddenly, with a bellowed 'Out!' a huge carle would swing his battleaxe, cleaving both horse and rider and bringing them crashing to the ground in a welter of blood and bone. Soon the lines had to move, almost imperceptibly, as the piles of dead made fighting ever harder, and corpses were dragged back to give the front lines room to carry on the struggle. The stink was terrible, blood mixing with sweat, urine and faeces on the now-slippery slopes of Battle Hill.

But William's tactics were working. The exhausted carles, England's vital élite, were being cut down, one at a time, and gaps began to appear in those crucial, heavily-armoured front ranks. Gradually, more poorly-equipped select fyrd men were forced to step forward into a front rank that was beginning to visibly shorten along the ridgeline. The fyrdmen were brave and relatively well trained, but they were not housecarles, and William knew it. Their padded leather jerkins were no substitute for the thousands of interwoven mail links of a hauberk, and Norman arrows and throwing spears punched home, killing them by the dozen and forcing more of their brethren into the wavering line. It was now that the superbly drilled Norman cavalry came into their own, each officer, the so-called *magister militum* (master of knights) calling out commands by voice, trumpet call or flag – the *gonfanons*. Seeing that sections of the shield wall were now manned by fyrdmen and not carles, the cavalry used their tactic of the feigned flight, pretending to fall away in disarray. Each time, considerable numbers of fyrdmen, freed from the horror of absorbing the punishment of the shield wall, sallied out, hoping to smash their opponents once and for all, only to see their fleeing quarry suddenly wheel around, cut them off from their comrades on the summit and surround them with a wall of horseflesh and chain-mail armour. William of Poitiers writes: 'Twice the Normans used this ruse with equal success,' and each time hundreds of Saxons were butchered on the blood-slicked grassy slopes. By now the English had just about run out of anything to throw at the Normans, every arrow, spear, javelin, hand axe and rock having been sent flying into their ranks. More importantly, the corps of housecarles was dying. Many had arrived at Hastings carrying wounds and injuries from Stamford Bridge, their armour saving their lives but unable to protect them from the broken bones and heavy bruising wrought by sword blows. Nevertheless, they had ridden at their earls' and king's command, their discipline paramount, bandaging arms and legs and tethering their mounts to take their place of honour in the line. They had not wavered, nor sallied out like their select fyrd comrades, but they were too few and they knew it. Most of them were lying where they had fallen, in the front rank, surrounded by the corpses of their foes.

But it wasn't over yet. The main body of the English army was still intact. True, the housecarles were nearly a spent force, but there were still numbers of professional lithsmen and the bravery of the several thousand select fyrdmen was undiminished. By now it was late afternoon, well after 3pm and it would be dark in less than two hours. Practised eyes looked around the battlefield, counting the numbers, grimly assessing the odds, and the truth was that only time could now save the English army, and both the remaining carles and William recognised it. If Harold could hold until nightfall, he would win. Cloaked by night, he would be able to take his men north, back to their horses on Caldbec Hill and the safety of the Andredsweald. There he could wait for reinforcements, especially Morcar and Edwin's northern levies who were marching south at that very moment. As for William, his men would have no choice but to retreat back to their encampment of the previous night knowing the dawn would bring them no such relief. There were no fresh men or mounts on their way to the Normans. The battle had now lasted an unbelievable six hours, and it still hung in the balance.

For the fourth and last time that day, it was William, not Harold, who acted decisively. Forsaking the rolling attacks of the last few hours, he ordered an all-out assault. The cavalry and infantry were to crash into the shield wall, all the while the archers were told to loose endless volleys into the hard-pressed English. William of Poitiers said of the English line, 'It was still terrifying to behold,' and so 'the Normans shot arrows, hit and pierced the enemy' and without hauberks man after man went down peppered with goose feather-fletched arrows. The Tapestry shows the remaining English warriors' shields thick with them.

The Norman horsemen tried to force their way through into the English line, that same line responding with equal ferocity. The legion of housecarles was not extinct just yet, and those that lived stood their ground, the axe-men still swinging away, shearing through armoured men and horses alike, the war-cry of 'Out, out, out', still defiant, but getting more ragged and fainter, shouted from parched mouths. Almost all the front line were now select fyrd and lithsmen. Instinct prompted most of the surviving carles to inch backwards to gather together around their lords and their banners, even now looking to protect them from what was to come, and leaving yet more lithsmen and fyrdmen to take their places in the shield wall. The dead were piled up in heaps, men standing among their own slaughtered comrades, no-one was pulling the corpses away now, and all eyes were on the advancing Normans.

Now, for the first time, lack of numbers forced the English line to retreat from the far western and eastern edges of the ridge, and the attacking Normans could see the shield wall perceptibly shrinking before them, its ranks getting thinner and thinner as the last of the carles in the frontlines were bludgeoned to death. There was no longer a dam of mail-shirts and huge battleaxes. Norman cavalry and infantry seized a foothold on the western end of the summit of Battle Hill, and could now attack straight into the English flank, forcing the shield wall to curve round to try and protect itself. It was the beginning of the end. The Normans could sense victory at long last. 'The longer they fought the stronger they seemed to be, and their onslaught was even fiercer now than it had been at the beginning' (Poitiers).

It was getting dark but it was too late, the lithsmen were almost all gone while the fyrd men were dying in droves, their courage not enough to compensate for their lack of armour and training. Then, suddenly, the once-continuous shield wall shivered and then shattered into pieces. In the mêlée that followed, the English army broke up into a myriad of small shield-rings. Desperate defenders circled their lords, stabbing with tired arms at the rejuvenated Normans who could smell victory. The biggest knot of fighters was, of course, grouped around the King himself, his twin standards still fluttering in the breeze. The men who still stood with Harold were his very best. These were the housecarles, lithsmen and thegns who had marched with the Godwinson family for 20 years and more. These men would not surrender and they continued to fight toe to toe with the Normans, while the majority of surviving fyrdmen fled for their lives, desperate to reach their tethered horses back on Caldbec Hill and ride for the safety of the Andredsweald a few miles north.

The English were beaten, but all was not yet lost. If Harold could escape then Anglo-Saxon England would still have a king and a rallying point. His survival was paramount and William knew it; Harold apparently did not. The Normans pressed home their attack, determined to achieve complete victory and wipe out the enemy who had held them at bay for so long, and without the protection of the war-hedge there was only death. Standing in the circle with their elder brother the King, the earls Leofwine and Gyrth were cut down and killed.

The Tapestry has them slain by the lances of heavy cavalry as Leofwine wields an axe, his brother a spear, both of them standing their ground. Between them the two brothers had controlled almost all of East Anglia and south-eastern England, and with them died all of their housecarles and personal retinues, their bodies falling about their lords. Harold was now the only English leader of note left alive on the battlefield. Why did he not flee in the gathering dark? Was he already dead, or mortally wounded and unable to seek safety? Confusingly the contemporary chronicler, William of Jumièges, wrote, 'Harold himself was slain, pierced with mortal wounds during the first assault.' Was the king actually dead during most of the battle, or maybe badly injured? This would at the very least explain his total inaction at every turn. Yet it seems unlikely that thousands of carles, paid lithsmen and fyrdmen would have stood and absorbed hours of savage punishment from the Normans with their king already dead, so we must discount this theory.

Far more likely is that Harold, as an exceptional warrior leader in his forties with more than 20 years experience, who had never known anything but victory, refused to believe he was defeated. Standing beneath his banners the King was now swinging his sword alongside his beloved Wessex housecarles, men with whom he had trained and fought since he was a boy. These men would not leave him, and whilst he stayed so did they. It was folly, and William punished it, a solid wedge of Norman cavalry smashing into Harold and his last few housecarles, cutting and slashing, and finally overwhelming the King and his remaining men.

Harold may or may not have been hit in the eye by a Norman arrow, but whatever the truth of that popular belief, inspired

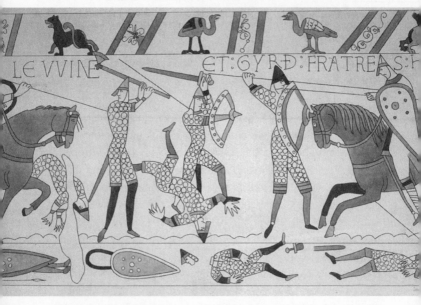

56. The battle nears its end, and Harold's brothers, Earl Leofwine and Earl Gyrth, are killed.

by the Bayeux Tapestry, he was killed in that final all-out attack and his body was hacked to pieces. With his death, the Battle of Hastings was lost, as was Anglo-Saxon England.

With English resistance utterly broken, William gave orders for his cavalry to set off in pursuit and turn defeat into a total rout. Fanning out from Battle Hill summit, the Franco-Norman horsemen charged off into the gathering gloom, cutting down the fleeing Saxons by the hundred, 'Many died where they fell in the deep cover of the woods' (Poitiers) as Hastings became a massacre. But with victory came complacency, and in the darkness a large contingent of Norman cavalry did not see Oakwood Gill, a steep ravine in front of them near Caldbec Hill, its sides and bottom choked with thick undergrowth. Tired horses tumbled down the slope, 'crushing each other to death' and several groups of surviving fyrdmen, who still had some fight left in them,

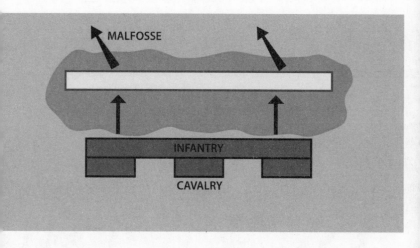

swarmed into the gully and butchered the helpless Normans. Battle Abbey's own chronicler wrote of the incident:

> …just where the fighting was going on, and stretching for a considerable distance, an immense ditch yawned. It may have been a natural cleft in the earth or perhaps it had been hollowed out by storms. But in this waste ground it was overgrown with brambles and thistles, and could hardly be seen in time, and it swallowed great numbers, especially of Normans in pursuit of the English.

The Normans called it the *Malfosse* – the 'evil ditch', and the setback there was enough to make William call off the pursuit and finally end the day's carnage. A battle had been fought and a country won and lost.

In retrospect it is doubtful whether any other state in Europe could have achieved what Anglo-Saxon England did in contesting three major battles in quick succession, but in the end it was all too much. There is little doubt that had Harold only faced either Norway or Normandy he would have kept his crown, but facing both was a task too great for even England's plentiful resources.

57. King Harold's death at the Battle of Hastings, the most controversial scene from the Bayeux Tapestry. Is Harold the figure struck by an arrow, or the one chopped down by the sword of a cavalryman? Or both? Indeed, is the first figure struck by the arrow, or is he simply holding it?

Edwin and Morcar's defeat at Fulford was a disaster for Harold, and the springboard for William's victory a month later. In one sense Hardrada's Norsemen were foot soldiers in the Norman army, though they did not know it, but it was they who destroyed the greater part of the considerable military might of the earldoms of Northumbria and Mercia; what few forces remained north of the Severn-Wash line died on the banks of the Derwent at Stamford Bridge alongside hundreds of Harold's own Wessex household troops, all of them men he could not afford to lose. Given a few months to rest and recover, England's resilient military structure could have replaced most of its losses, and William would then

NEW WORLD SALVATION

Battle Abbey and the battle-site itself was owned by the Church and in the 1970s its future was in doubt due to the enormous cost of upkeep. Salvation came from the unlikely source of the United States, from where a group of donors, many of them anonymous, gave Her Majesty's Government a large sum of money to purchase both the Abbey and the land, and preserve it for posterity on the anniversary of the USA's bicentennial. A plaque commemorating this gesture can be found in the gatehouse of the Abbey.

have faced an army that outnumbered him two to one or more, its fyrdmen simply overwhelming his own troops through sheer weight of numbers. Instead, by dashing south without lingering to gather more men, Harold's shield wall at Hastings was far smaller than it should have been and simply not big enough to counter William's more sophisticated tactics and use of all-arms. The Earl of Wessex and King of England was undone in the end by lack of armour, the men who wore it, and knowing how to use them to their best advantage. In truth Harold Godwinson was simply outgeneraled and outnumbered.

AFTER THE BATTLE

The outcome of Hastings was totally unequivocal; Duke William, his fellow Normans and their French allies were the overwhelming winners, while King Harold, the Godwinsons and the rest of the existing Anglo-Scandinavian nobility of England lost everything. Most obviously King Harold II was dead, and was replaced by King William I. With William came Normandy, and streams of men from northern France, all seeking their fortune at the expense of the native Anglo-Saxons and their Scandinavian brethren.

Hastings marks the biggest break in the leadership of England in all of our island's history; far greater than the effects of the Roman invasions or even the waves of Anglo-Saxon and Viking raiders and settlers that followed centuries later. The Danish King Canute had come to the throne of a disunited land composed of a multitude of ancient kingdoms, the most powerful being Wessex, Mercia and Northumbria, with East Anglia and Kent as semi-autonomous 'statelets', and he had brought them together into a single, centrally-governed, entity, reducing those independent kingdoms down to earldoms, and bringing them firmly under the crown's authority.

But England was still far from being a united country, and the populace still saw themselves either as Mercians, Northumbrians or West Saxons. 1066 changed all that, with Mercia and

58. A Victorian depiction of the Battle of Hastings.

Northumbria beaten to their knees at the Battle of Fulford, before they were truly lost at Hastings along with Wessex, Kent and East Anglia. Their ruling houses were crushed, as was every layer of English leadership from north to south, and in time even their names would fade into oblivion, their ancient heritage turned to ashes.

Edwin of Mercia and his brother Morcar of Northumbria, their power broken at Fulford and Stamford Bridge, did not reach Hastings in time to fight and so survived to surrender to William in Berkhamsted before the end of the year. Morcar lost his earldom, William giving it to Tostig's lieutenant, Copsi. His brother Edwin was killed in 1071, and his northern estates, centred at Gilling

EDWIN AND MORCAR

After their submission at Berkhamsted, Edwin and Morcar soon realised there was no place for them in William's Norman England and the two of them raised Mercia in revolt in 1068. They failed miserably, submitted, and were pardoned. Still discontented, three years later they again sought to rebel, but Edwin was betrayed by his own retinue and murdered. Morcar ended up joining the last great English rebellion led by Hereward the Wake on the Isle of Ely. When the Isle fell he was captured and imprisoned. He remained in prison until William's death in 1087, whereupon he enjoyed a brief period of freedom before the new king, William Rufus, had him locked up again. Morcar, Earl of Northumbria, son of Aelfgar Earl of Mercia, grandson of Leofric Earl of Mercia, died in captivity shortly after, a broken man.

West, were given to the Norman Alain Le Roux. The district was renamed Richmondshire.

The Godwinsons, the most influential family in the land and rulers of all of southern England, were now more or less extinct. Godwin's eldest son Swein had died years before on pilgrimage of course, Tostig was killed at Stamford Bridge, and Harold, Leofwine and Gyrth all perished at Hastings. Harold's body was so badly mutilated as to be unrecognisable. In the end his long-time mistress, Edith Swan-neck, was the only one able to identify him, the legend being that she could make out 'intimate markings', perhaps a tattoo of Wessex's famed Wyvern emblem. Harold's mother tried to buy the body from William and ensure a proper burial, but naturally the Duke feared it would become a focal point for English resistance and refused. William of Poitiers writes: 'His [King Harold's] corpse was brought into the Duke's camp and William gave it for burial to William, surnamed Malet, and not to Harold's mother, who offered for the body of her beloved son its weight in gold.'

59. *Waltham Abbey Church. This ancient church and its peaceful grounds sit in the midst of the modern town. Part of the wall nearest to Harold's gravesite is from the original Saxon building.*

60. *King Harold II's memorial in the grounds of Waltham Abbey church. The plaque reads: 'This stone marks the position of the high altar behind which King Harold is said to have been buried, 1066.' Every 14 October people gather here to remember him and lay flowers.*

WALTHAM ABBEY

The site of King Harold's eventual gravesite, Waltham Abbey has been a church since the seventh century and was re-built in stone by Harold himself after he was 'cured' of paralysis after praying to a famous holy cross brought there from Somerset. His gravestone lies outside the east end of the building and is still a place of pilgrimage with people gathering on the anniversary of his death to lay flowers in remembrance of England's last Anglo-Saxon monarch. A memorial to the family of the Anglo-Saxon rebel, Hereward the Wake, is also in the church on the south wall. The original community of 13 secular canons established by Harold was increased in 1177 when Henry II enlarged the church as part of his penance for the murder of Thomas Beckett.

Initially buried in an unmarked grave near the sea, William later relented and the body was taken to the abbey church at Waltham Cross that Harold had generously endowed when he was the Earl of Wessex. There he was quietly interred.

Of Godwin's six sons only the youngster Waltheof was still alive after 14 October 1066, still held hostage by William as he had been since he was a young boy. Harold's own offspring, three by Edith and two by his wife Ealdgyth, scattered. Most escaped abroad, while some of the older boys attacked England's south-west from a base in Ireland to try and stir up rebellion and regain their father's throne, but their attempts were doomed to failure and they faded from the pages of history to die in obscurity.

Lying alongside the Godwinsons on Battle Hill, their bones bleaching white and sinking into the sandy earth, were probably well over 4000 other Englishmen. Half of them were England's famed housecarles. These were the men who had saved England from the Vikings for over 200 years and were renowned throughout Europe for their martial prowess and courage. Harold had gambled on them at Hastings to hold the line and beat the

WHERE ARE THE GRAVE PITS?

Whilst this book tries to encapsulate the most likely events of 1066 acording to the latest thinking and research, part of the fascincation of the battle is that we still cannot be sure of so much. By about 1900 a consensus had been reached that the battle was fought by two sides of roughly equal number around the crest of the Battle Abbey ridge. Whilst we cannot prove this untrue, equally, we cannot prove that it is certain. No graves have been discovered to authenticate either the numbers or the location. Was the battle fought over a larger area, perhaps, contradicting the original sources we have?

Norman cavalry, and though they had failed they had remained true to their vows of loyalty. Hastings was their death-knell, and they were wiped out almost to a man, never to be reformed. Amongst the heaps of corpses, and lying next to the housecarles, were vast swathes of Anglo-Saxon England's nobility; its lesser earls, lords and thegns – men whose families had held land for centuries and were the very bedrocks of their communities. William of Poitiers:

> …once he had completed his victory, the duke rode back to the battlefield to survey the dead. It was impossible to contemplate them without being moved to pity … the flower of English youth and nobility littered the ground far and wide.

These men had provided England with its governing class for centuries, and now they were shattered, hundreds of them lying slaughtered around their king on the battlefield. The few that survived were dispossessed and brushed aside by the conquerors. Back in Cocking, the fate of its own Saxon thegn Azor is inscribed on a bronze pillar raised to commemorate the history of the village: '1066 – Azor, last Saxon governor ousted by Normans.'

RUSSIAN DESCENDANTS

As the few remaining Godwinsons scattered to the four winds, Godwin and Gytha's daughter, also called Gytha, ended up marrying the Scandinavian Prince Vladimir II of Kiev – one of the famous *Rus*. Their descendants would go on to help found Russia and rule over it for centuries until Moscow's ascendancy and the rise of the House of Romanov.

This act of dispossession was repeated across the length and breadth of England after the Conquest, so that 20 years after Hastings, when the entire country was surveyed, the effects of Hastings were plain for all to see. This incredible piece of work covered 13,148 English cities, towns, villages and hamlets in total and came to be known as the 'Domesday Book' by the populace, as they realised it spelt nothing but despair for them and their traditional way of life; or more accurately, it embodied the truth that only two things are sure in this life – death and taxes. Richard FitzNigel wrote around 1179 that the book was named after the Day of Judgement because 'as the sentence of that strict and terrible last account cannot be evaded by any skilful subterfuge, so when this book is appealed to ... its sentence cannot be quashed or set aside with impunity ... its decisions, like those of the Last Judgment, are unalterable.' The book was William's attempt to assess the country's wealth and hence raise more taxes, and in that he succeeded.

The Domesday Book also provides us with a mass of detail on the fate of England's landowning classes after Hastings, including, of course, Azor and Cocking:

Robert FitzTheobald [Norman] holds Cocking of Earl Roger de Montgomerie [Norman]. Azor held it of King Edward. Assessed at 12 hides [a hide was a measure of land used in the

61. *The memorial built to mark the spot where King Harold supposedly fell.*

south for about 120 acres]. Land for 11 and a half ploughs. There is a church, six slaves and five mills rendering 37 shillings and sixpence.

To the victor the spoils. The Normans and their allies fell on England with gusto. Hastings had been a bloody day for them too, with as many as 2000 or more dying before the shield wall, and those that were left were determined to seize their reward. William was equally determined they should receive it, and he gave them carte blanche to take as they wished.

First and foremost the duke had to secure the crown he had won in blood at Hastings. The King, his carles, and most of the nobility of England lay rotting on Battle Hill, but the country was far from conquered. William possessed no major city, the northern lords were still alive and free, and there was even an Atheling, Edgar, who could threaten the fruits of the day. William's plan was masterly. Splitting his army into strong, self-contained columns he began a 'procession' through southern England, centred on that most powerful English city, London. Swarming across the populous south-east the Normans stamped on any embers of resistance, dealing harshly with anyone who raised a hand against them. Villages were burned, crops confiscated, and motte and bailey fortifications erected everywhere as a demonstration of Norman dominance.

There were still potentially droves of fighting men left in England, the housecarles might have been annihilated but the select fyrd could still number thousands of men, let alone the untrained masses of the great fyrd. There were also significant numbers of lithsmen and other Scandinavian mercenaries, mostly in the north, who were ready as ever to fight for whoever would pay them. It was true that these contingents would lack the quality of the veteran Norman cavalry and heavy infantry, but as Stalin once famously remarked, 'Quantity has a quality all of its own.' But what Anglo-Saxon England lacked far more than mail-shirted professional warriors was the men who would lead them.

62. The ruins of Berkhamsted Castle where Archbishop Stigand brought the Atheling Edgar and the Earls Edwin and Morcar to submit to William. The Anglo-Saxon Chronicle considered 'it was a great piece of folly that they had not done it earlier.'

The death of the ruling class at Hastings robbed England of its capacity to resist and William's ensuing actions capitalised on that. After ravaging the south, the very man who had placed the crown on Harold's head, Archbishop Stigand of Canterbury, gathered the remnants of Anglo-Saxon England's leaders – the Earls Edwin and Morcar foremost among them – at Berkhamsted, northwest of London and there in December 1066 they surrendered and submitted to William as their rightful ruler and king.

England did not have a single leader of note left and when William advanced on London he easily crushed the token resistance put up by the greatest city in the land. Then, in Westminster Abbey, on Christmas Day, almost exactly a year to the day since Harold Godwinson was himself enthroned as King of England, the crown was placed on William's head by Archbishop Ealdred of York. He ceased to be Duke William the Bastard of Normandy, and became King William I of England, the Conqueror.

King William and his men knew though that they were strangers in a strange land, and the new monarch realised he needed more allies and more of his own kind. The Franco-Normans were still a very small minority of less than 5000 amongst a sea of Saxons, so the call went out back across the Channel that riches were to be had in the newly conquered country. Over the next 20 years as many as 30–40,000 more Normans, Bretons, Flemings, Poitevins and northern French landed in England to help solidify the Conquest. The ownership of land, the basis of all wealth in medieval England, was utterly transformed, and the biggest winners from this massive land grab were the victors of Hastings.

Firstly came William himself and his extended family, who had seized a full 20 per cent of England's entire acreage by 1087. His half-brother Robert, the Count of Mortain, was granted the rape of Pevensey (a rape was a traditional sub-division of Sussex) and the massive total of 549 manors scattered across the country: 54 in Sussex, 75 in Devon, 49 in Dorset, 29 in Buckinghamshire, 13 in Hertfordshire, 10 in Suffolk, 99 in Northamptonshire, 196 in Yorkshire, and 24 in other counties. The greatest concentration of his landed wealth was in Cornwall (where he held a further 248 manors at the time of the compilation of the Domesday Book, together with the castles of Launceston and Trematon) although these Cornish estates were not granted to him until after 1072 when their previous holder, Brian of Brittany, decided to return home. Robert was eventually was made the 1st Earl of Cornwall, before dying in 1095.

A further 25 per cent of the country was in the hands of the Church (the Norman church of course), and 50 per cent was held by just 190 of William's Franco-Norman supporters acting as tenants-in-chief to the king. Only one major pre-Conquest magnate, the Anglo-Danish *jarl* Thorkill of Arden, still held his Warwickshire estates by the same year. In all, only 5 per cent

... JOIN THEM

Despite being supported at times by Edwin, Morcar, and much of England's remaining Anglo-Saxon aristocracy, the only surviving member of the ancient Cerdician line of kings, Edgar the Atheling, never made any real bid for the crown. Content with England's new rulers, and forgetting his own people, he became a Norman lackey and even accompanied William the Conqueror's eldest son Robert on crusade to Jerusalem.

of England was left in the hands of Saxons and Scandinavians according to Domesday. The new barons ate off silver plate in their castles, while the few remaining Anglo-Saxon thegns were lucky to be relegated to under-tenant status, their lands and privileges taken from their grasp with no recompense.

William's Companions, the men he had elevated in Normandy to be the backbone of his rule, were granted unimaginable wealth and became the great magnates of England, many of whose families are still prominent today. Men like Richard FitzGilbert who was given land in Kent, Surry, Suffolk and Norfolk and built castles at Tonbridge in Kent, Bletchingley in Surrey, Hanley in Worcestershire and the most famous at Clare in Suffolk. So renowned did he become for that particular castle that he took it as his family name and was thereafter called 'Richard de Clare'. Another Companion, Walter Giffard, Lord of Longueville, had led his men against the last of the housecarles on the summit of Battle Hill, riding them down and crushing their resistance. His reward was the feudal honour of Crendon in Buckinghamshire. Over time his land holdings increased, so that under William Rufus he was made the 1st Earl of Buckingham, a title he passed to his son, also called Walter, on his death around 1100. Others included William de Warenne, the 1st Earl of Surrey, William Malet (he who had initially buried King Harold's body at Hastings) created Lord of Graville, Roger de Beaumont (who commanded a cohort of

A SUBSTANTIAL MORTAL COIL

William was an old man of 60 when he died. Grown enormously fat, the king was back in Normandy protecting his duchy from the belligerent French king. William defeated the French army and burnt the city of Mantes to the ground. Following the victory his horse stumbled and William was badly injured in the gut. Taken to a monastery near Rouen he died a few days later. The attendant nobles panicked and left the king's corpse unattended. Thieves stole in and stripped it, and then when burial was finally attempted his abundance of mortal flesh would not fit the special stone casket and the stench of decay hung over the ceremony.

Normans in Count Alan's vanguard at Battle Hill) was made the 1st Earl of Leicester, William fitz Osbern, the 1st Earl of Hereford and so on. Hugh de Montfort, Lord of Montfort-sur-Risle, Ralph de Tosny, Lord of Conches, Hugh de Grandmesnil, Turstin fitzRolf, Engenulf de Laigle, Geoffrey de Mortagne, later Count of Perche, and Aimeri, Viscount of Thouars – these men received the lands, wealth and titles of the men they slew at Hastings, and their descendants took the power of Norman arms across the Mediterranean and the Middle East.

As for the Conqueror himself, he had risen from being the hunted, bastard son of a minor French nobleman to become the anointed ruler of one of the richest and most powerful kingdoms in Europe. He would reign for over 20 years and by the time he died on 9 September 1087 his family was secure on the throne and Anglo-Saxon England was gone forever.

THE LEGACY

There are few battles in history that can truly be called epoch-making, they are indeed rare and must be judged in the fullness of history – Hastings is one such battle. In the space of a single day the whole future of England was changed forever, and the history of the world re-shaped as a result. As such it ranks alongside the likes of Thermopylae, Waterloo, Hattin and Stalingrad.

A young country, still finding its feet as a nation, England had seemed set on becoming part of the Viking world, tied across the expanse of the North Sea with Norway, Denmark and Sweden and the expanding Scandinavian sphere of influence. The country was well balanced, with the north of England as economically, politically and culturally powerful as the south. Instead, in a few years, the north would be reduced to ashes, never to fully recover, as England's focus was forcibly wrenched to the south, the country looking to western, rather than northern, Europe. Huge numbers of Anglo-Saxon England's traditional leaders were either slaughtered or supplanted, and a rigid class divide was put in place, with not even a common language to unite them. Anglo-Saxon England was not some paradise lost, burnt to the ground by rapacious Normans, but it is true to say that the country was changed irrevocably, more outward looking across the Channel and to the east, growing in power, wealth and influence, but also perhaps less at ease with itself, with a chasm between the rulers and the ruled that still defines British society even today.

Before 1066, England's fate had been dominated by invaders from across the sea for close on 1000 years. First it had been Rome and her legions, crossing from Gaul, consigning Celtic Britain to oblivion, and tying the island into an expansionist southern European empire centred on the Mediterranean. The barbarian migrations of the fourth and fifth centuries severed that link, and over time shifted the land's gravity across the North Sea as waves of Germanic invaders set out for England's shores from modern-day Germany, Denmark and the Low Countries of Belgium and the Netherlands. Anglo-Saxon England, as it became, maintained its strong ties across the sea, but also developed an identity of its own, as you would expect from an island nation.

The arrival of the Vikings some 300 years later then cemented England's focus on Europe's northern rim, as Scandinavia tried to draw England permanently into its grasp. This era reached its height with Canute's accession to the throne and England's incorporation into a Scandinavian empire alongside Denmark, Norway, the Orkneys and Shetlands, the Hebrides and much of Scotland. Harald Hardrada's Norwegian invasion of northern England was simply a continuation of this centuries-old struggle that began with the sacking of Lindisfarne and the killing of the king's reeve at Portland. The defeat of the brothers Edwin and Morcar at Fulford confirmed to the country that it was indeed the Vikings who posed the greater threat to England's security, with William and his Normans seen as a far lesser danger. After all, the majority of the nobility, including the King himself, had Scandinavian blood running through their veins, Viking law ruled in the Danelaw and there were very large numbers of Danish and Norwegian settlements in the country; the likes of Askrigg, Aysgarth, Husthwaite and Burtersett being but a few ('thwaite' is the Norse word for 'clearing', while 'sett' means 'summer hut'). Even that most famous of Yorkshire words, 'dale', is Viking, being the Norse for 'valley'.

Not that the new settlers did not mix with the native Anglo-Saxons. Scandinavian women did join their menfolk, bringing their language and way of life to England, but a large number of the new raiders and settlers were young men who were only too happy to marry local girls and watch as their children learnt Saxon-English at their mother's breast. The Anglo-Saxon word for a farm – 'ton'- is still ubiquitous across northern England, with Ingleton, Skipton and Horton being a few of the thousands of places with the suffix. (The latter by the way literally means 'farm-in- the-mud'.)

It was common wisdom that it would take just one more push from across the sea and Canute's days would return, and with it an age for England as 'new Scandinavia'. King Harold's victory at Stamford Bridge caused that possible future to recede, but did not in itself shatter it. Saxon England had won great victories against the Vikings before; Alfred at Edington and Athelstan at Brunanburh to name but two, yet still the ravenous northmen had always returned. The destruction of the huge Norwegian army outside York simply left the field open for King Svein Esthrithson's Denmark to try its luck, and try it would, but to no avail. England was no longer betwixt and between, it was a Norman country, united by a powerful, martial royal family and nobility that brooked no opposition. It was tied to the south, to France, and to dreams of conquest and empire in warmer climes, as far east as the Garden of Gethsemane and the Mount of Olives. Svein's Denmark was no match for such a country, and although William had to buy off the Danes occasionally, it was more from convenience than weakness. In the end, Hastings spelt the doom of Viking England far more than Stamford Bridge.

As much as Hastings was the end of Viking England, it was also the 'demise' of the region the Scandinavians had long seen as a home from home – England's rugged north. Today we are used to the hegemony of London and England's south-east corner; their economic, political and cultural domination of our island is complete, even the source of humour. While this divide seems natural to us now, this was not the case in 1066. York ranked alongside the royal capital of Winchester itself as the second biggest city in the country, and almost an alternative capital, especially for the Anglo-Vikings who had looked to York/Jorvik for decades anyway. The north was very wealthy, its farmland rich and fertile, its trade strong in goods such as wool and jewellery, and its nobility powerful and independent. Fulford was indeed a hammer blow to the north, as was Stamford Bridge, but they were far from being terminal ones. Hastings and its aftermath was an altogether different matter. When much of southern England surrendered at Berkhamsted in the winter of 1066, the heart went out of English resistance across the lands from the Wash to the Severn, not so in the north. The Normans had hardly been seen in the old earldoms of Mercia and Northumbria, and they had won no military victory there either. The surviving local nobility looked for support across the North Sea back to the Scandinavian homelands, and discontent in the north at Norman rule was endemic. The Normans then only inflamed northern resentment with their high-handed behaviour and insensitive rule, as the Anglo-Saxon Chronicle recorded: '… they built castles far and wide throughout the land, oppressing the unhappy people, and things went ever from bad to worse.'

Allying with the Danes and their King, the opportunistic Svein, the north rose in revolt and in January 1069 killed their newly-appointed Norman overlord, Robert de Comines, and all his men in a massacre in the city of Durham. De Comines had been appointed after William's first choice as Earl of Northumbria, Copsi, had fallen foul of the locals and been murdered by Osulf, son of Eadulf III of the ancient Bernician ruling family —which had historically governed the area from Bamburgh – after being earl for a mere five weeks. Osulf himself only lasted a few months as he was killed in turn by an outlaw he was tracking. William had had enough of northern unruliness and de Comines was instructed to pacify the region. His death was viewed by the king as a deliberate challenge to his rule, and his response was both immediate and almost genocidal. Buying the Danes and Svein off with his own version of Danegeld, William went on to smash the rebels and

63. Across England, the Normans built. This is Brough Castle in Cumbria, originally the Roman fort of Verteris. The Norman Clifford family held it for centuries.

then decided to settle the northern question once and for all. His new policy has gone down in history as the infamous 'Harrying of the North', and would effectively condemn its people to centuries of impoverishment. Orderic recalls William's orders:

> ... he ordered the corn and cattle, with the implements of husbandry and every sort of provision, be collected in heaps and set on fire until the whole was consumed, and thus destroyed at once all that could serve for the support of life in the whole country lying beyond the Humber.

The destruction was on a truly epic scale, with the entire region between the Humber and the Tees rivers laid to waste, and even much of northern Mercia did not escape the King's wrath. Thousands were butchered by the Norman soldiery, their homes burnt, their crops stolen or despoiled. All Livestock was driven south or slaughtered and wells were poisoned. Entire villages and towns were ransacked, any who resisted were put to the sword, and then the thatch was set alight and the survivors driven out into the surrounding countryside with no means of support. The capital of northern England, the ancient and beautiful city of York, was torched. The people fled for their lives and the city went into decline, with some 940 of the city's 1400 houses still derelict almost 20 years later. For those who were spared, life simply got even worse. With nothing to eat and no means of growing food or farming, starvation set in and killed thousands. Weakened by lack of food and shelter, diseases spread like wildfire; even cannibalism was reported among the wretched survivors. The monks of Evesham wrote of columns of ragged refugees streaming south away from the destruction, some so weak and malnourished that they died as they arrived at the churchyard. It is impossible to accurately gauge the total casualties, however it is probable that as many as 100,000 inhabitants of Mercia and Northumbria died from the sword, famine and disease.

Overall, the population of the north and much of the midlands crashed. By the time of the Domesday Book there were fewer than three people per square mile living in the north, compared to ten in the southeast and East Anglia. The value of land plummeted by more than a quarter as there was no-one left alive to work it. Records eloquently describe the wholesale nature of the campaign, for instance, of Northallerton in Yorkshire, held by Earl Edwin of Mercia, Domesday says: 'There were 116 sokemen [freemen]. Now it is waste.' Of Falsgrave and Northfield (near Scarborough): 'there were 108 sokemen, now there are 7 sokemen and 15 villeins (*serfs*). The rest are waste.' From my own region of south Yorkshire, Domesday says of Penistone: 'Alric [Saxon] had 10 bovates of land to the geld, and there could be 1 carucate [a tax assessment of land in the north meaning the amount of land that a team of 8 oxen could plough] of land. Now the same man has it of Ilbert de Lacy [Norman] and it is waste.'

In all, an astounding half of the land in the north was recorded as 'waste' after the Harrying, and while the rest of England was watched over by a network of Norman motte and bailey castles, there were hardly any built in Yorkshire – there was simply no-one left to cow. Even the church was not immune from the punishment, and William ordered that the See of York would no longer be equal to Canterbury, but would be its junior. Northern England would not be important again for another 800 years and the coming of the Industrial Revolution.

William did not impose an alien class system on an Anglo-Saxon England that had previously been some sort of idyllic Garden of Eden, where all were equal and Adam delve and Eve span. English society was already stratified in 1066 with a hereditary aristocracy and layers of power and privilege – Azor held Cocking just as his father and grandfather did – albeit with porous boundaries allowing a sometimes astonishing degree of social mobility – after all, King Harold himself was a commoner whose grandfather was little more than the leader of a handful of warriors. William's Normandy too was a land of 'new men', with the duke creating an aristocracy centred on his Companions, who were nothing before his accession to the dukedom. However, the Normans' total supplanting of the existing ruling class and domination of all the levers of power, their unwillingness to assimilate into English society and above all, their use of their own language and culture to denote superiority over the English, were the real beginnings of hostile class divide in England. From then on everything Anglo-Saxon was portayed as brutish and coarse and to be generally despised, and this legacy is still with us today; anyone who speaks of 'England' is disparaged as a 'little Englander' with all its connatations of ignorance and vulgarity, while those who look towards the Continent are regarded as sophisticated and somehow superior. This is nowhere clearer than in the very richness of the English language itself. 'William' soon became the most popular boy's name in the land. With English mothers and wet nurses, the sons and daughters of the Norman conquerors

64. *Colchester Castle, the largest surviving Norman keep in Western Europe. Built on the site of the Roman Temple of Juno, which was burned to the ground by Boudicca and her Iceni during their revolt, much of the stone was recycled and used by the Normans.*

RELATIVE SANCTITY OF HUMAN LIFE

For the first time in English history a 'racial' law was introduced by the Normans. Spurred on by the fact that the new Norman Abbot of Abingdon, Adelhelm, could only go about the countryside with armed guards, a law was drafted to protect the Normans from vengeful Saxons which stated that if a person was found murdered it was the responsibility of the local village to prove he was Saxon, if not he was considered to be a Norman and therefore killed unjustly and the villagers were heavily fined.

65. The Tower of London, an expression of Norman power.

grew up speaking Anglo-Saxon, but it was a different Anglo-Saxon than Alfred or even the Confessor would have recognised.

Traditional Anglo-Saxon was seen as primitive and uneducated, whereas the new French words were very much in vogue. Everyday food was Saxon when it was grubbing in the mud, words like 'pig', and 'sheep', but when clean, cooked and ready to eat it was French 'pork' and 'mutton'. The language of power was the same; Saxons spoke of 'kingly' and 'queenly', Normans of 'royal', 'authority', 'governing' and 'empire'. (They also brought the word 'torture'.) Alongside language the Normans built physical barriers between themselves and their new neighbours. Fortifications were not unknown in Anglo-Saxon England, but the arrival of the Normans utterly transformed England as the invaders covered the country in motte and baileys, keeps and huge castles. Hitherto the majority of fortresses, be they the ancient Celtic British hill forts or the Anglo-Saxon burhs, were partly constructed to enable the

66. View along the battlements of Lincoln Castle towards the keep. Nicola de la Haye kept the French and rebel forces out long enough for them to be defeated in 1217.

67. East gate of Lincoln Castle facing the cathedral. Retreating troops poured through this gate during the Second Battle of Lincoln. (Photographs courtesy Sean McGlynn from Blood Cries Afar)

150 YEARS LATER

Having built castles at Warwick, Nottingham and York to secure the North and the Midlands, William turned south. Lincoln represented a strategic crossroads, not least along Ermine street, a Roman road connecting York and London, and the Fosse Way, connecting Lincoln with Leicester and the south west. Work on the new castle was completed in 1068. Unusually, it had two mottes, the only other example of this being at Lewes. Remarkably enough, Lincoln Castle would be under siege almost exactly 150 years after the Battle of Hastings, when once more an invading force from France landed to claim the English throne. Louis the Lion, son of the French King, Philip Augustus, allied with the English barons in revolt against King John, managed to secure half the kingdom – including London – before John's timely death and a counter-attack by the royalists rallying around the infant Henry III prevented a second successful invasion. The full story of the astonishing invasion of 1216 is told in Sean McGlynn's *Blood Cries Afar*. Louis's forces were in control of Lincoln city but did not take the castle, the garrison of which remained loyal to Henry. The Battle of Lincoln in May 1217 saw the barons and their French allies defeated and the end of the war.

local populace to shelter from attack behind their protective walls. Not so the Norman edifices. They were not designed to welcome the people, but expressly to keep them out. The White Tower of London and Colchester castle were demonstrations of power, and a visible manifestation of the Norman view of ordinary Anglo-Saxons as a potentially dangerous threat. Almost a thousand years after William triumphed at Battle Hill, we are still living with the legacy of that bloody autumn day.

VISITING THE BATTLEFIELD

In trying to understand the Battle of Hastings and get a real sense of what happened and why, there is absolutely no substitute for visiting the battlefield itself. Now under the guardianship of English Heritage the site is well looked after and has numbers of knowledgeable volunteers and staff who are exceedingly helpful. An English visitor's only possible complaint would be having to pay money to walk it. Everyone in Britain has inherited what happened on that hill almost a millennium ago, and it can grate that we must pay to see it, but that must be balanced with the need to preserve the site and that inevitably takes money.

The greatest thing about walking the battlefield is exactly that – the ability to walk it. Having written on a number of twentieth-century conflicts, I find the sheer size of the sites daunting. Kharkiv and Cherkassy in the Ukraine are spread over tens of square miles, and even the Normandy landing sites of D-Day cover miles of beaches, towns, villages and countryside. Whereas Hastings can be walked from one end to the other and from top to bottom in ten minutes flat. That lack of scale is one of the most satisfying and illuminating revelations you will get from a visit. Standing there in the wet grass, feeling the sandy soil under your feet, looking at the bare expanse of the hill, the visitor realises the very nature of 14 October 1066. This was no battle of manoeuvre with generals based miles away shifting armies of men, fleets of aircraft and massed artillery and armour. The future of England and Normandy was fought out here by men who were staring into each other's eyes and could smell the stink of their opponents' breath. It is chilling and and I cannot recommend it highly enough, especially on 14 October itself when a large-scale re-enactment is staged.

The site is open most of the year, although only at weekends during the winter, and it is best to check on the website www. english-heritage.org.uk/battleabbey for details before travelling.

Visiting Stamford Bridge and Fulford is also to be recommended, although for different reasons. Whereas Hastings is commemorated and venerated, these twin Yorkshire battles have largely been forgotten, and a visit to the sites fills one with a terrible sadness at a nation with so much history that it can discard pieces of it like old newspapers.

The other site of interest is of course – www.tapestry-bayeux.com/ – the Bayeux Tapestry Museum. There is also a Victorian copy of at Reading Museum – www.bayeuxtapestry.org.uk/ – in England.

FURTHER READING

If the reader has the appetite for it I can recommend going to some of the original sources, such as Orderic Vitalis' *Historia Ecclesiastica*, written in the early 1100s and so very close to the events themselves. William of Poitiers' *Histoire de Guillaume le Conquérant* was written around 1072–74 by William's own chaplain, and so is necessarily biased in his favour; it nevertheless was based on first-hand accounts of men who were present on the day of the battle.

Domesday Book is now online, and no other work gives the reader such a sense of the aftermath of the Conquest, and naturally there is also the Bayeux Tapestry, a truly magnificent work of art and history. The Tapestry took about two years to complete and was designed for Bayeux's cathedral, consecrated in 1077. It is a miracle it has survived through the centuries, with dictators from Napoleon to Hitler coming close to destroying it.

Bradbury, Jim, *The Battle of Hastings* (Sutton Publishing, 1998)
Lawson, M.K., *The Battle of Hastings 1066* (Tempus Publishing, 2002)
Loyn, H.R., *Anglo-Saxon England and the Norman Conquest* (Longman, 1970)
Matthew, D.J.A., *The Norman Conquest* (B.T. Batsford, 1966)

Further Reading

McGlynn, Sean, *Blood Cries Afar: The Forgotten Invasion of England 1216* (Spellmount 2011)

Rex, Peter, *Harold II: The Doomed Saxon King* (Tempus Publishing, 2005)

Stenton, F.M., *William the Conqueror* (London, 1927)

Wise, Terence, *1066 Year of Destiny* (Osprey Publishing, 1979)

INDEX

Index

Index